Additional Praise for *Leading Fi*

• • •

"I find your new book, like you, to be inspiring. It is a common sense road map to success, including a theme from beginning to end about what you learned from Sam Walton of Wal-Mart."

    – Thomas V.H. Vail, Retired Publisher & Editor, The Plain Dealer

"I did have a chance to read your book, Leading From the Heart. I was inspired and could not put your book down. It touched on many ideas and beliefs that I have felt in my heart and some that I have done from day one. I learned a great deal and will recommend it to anyone who wants to grow in their profession."

    – Jim Paxson, President & General Manager, Cleveland Cavaliers

"Your text is a valuable addition to the libraries of men and women who thirst for direction, who wish to combine theory and practice to complete their learning experience, and who can be believers in what they read, due to the accomplishments of the author's own leadership. Well done, Dear Heart! (Your heart is such a huge one, you'd have to lead from it!)"

    – Michael A. Clegg, Retired President, Ostendorf-Morris

"We have read your draft of Leading From the Heart and must tell you that it should be required reading for anyone striving for success. Not just in business but in life. As you have illustrated in countless examples, unless 'heart' is in the equation, true success will not follow. Heart + Leadership = True Success."

    – John Nottingham & John Spirk, Nottingham Spirk Design Associates, Inc. ($25 billion of designed products sold to-date)

"Leading From the Heart provides great insight as to what is important about running a business. You have written your autobiography of leadership. You have combined basic elements of good leadership with quotes from intellectuals, philosophers, and military leaders. The combination is dynamite."

    – Carl Bellini, Retired CEO, Gray Drug & Retired President & COO, Revco Drug & Advisory Board Member, Henkel Consumer Adhesives

"Jack Kahl invites you in to Manco, where you will feel the heartbeat of every employee winning the Super Bowl for Jack year after year. Leading From the Heart is required reading for every business student in America."

    – Larry Morrow, Retired Radio Personality, WWWE & Owner, Larry Morrow Group

LEADING

FROM
THE

HEART

Choosing to be a Servant Leader

Jack Kahl

with Tom Donelan

Published in the United States by
Jack Kahl and Associates
26100 First Street
Logos Communications Building
Westlake, OH 44145

www.jackkahl. com

Layout and Cover Design by Francine Smith
Paperback Edition

This book is dedicated to all the partners (employees) of Manco, Inc. who put their heads, hearts, and hands to work to build a great team and company. My thanks to each of them for the privilege of being called their leader.

CONTENTS

ACKNOWLEDGEMENTS

It all begins with one little word: *thanks*.

I'd like to start by thanking my mom and dad and all my brothers and sisters for the great and loving home we grew up in; we had some good fights, but we also had a sense of teamwork and always cared for one another. There was always kindness and a selfless love, which we can all attribute to mom, the heart of our home.

To my teachers at St. Edward High School and John Carroll University who taught, challenged, and scared the hell out of me if I didn't perform. Special thanks to Art Noetzel, Dean of the Business School at John Carroll, who helped me to grow from boyhood to manhood with just a few cogent remarks.

Thanks also to Harold Linden, the man who helped me understand how to buy Manco way back in 1971. When he said, "Remember Jack, you do big business out of small places and don't reverse the formula," Harold gave me a business philosophy that I practice to this day. Because of Harold's great advice, we have always managed to stay efficient and keep our competitive edge.

I thank my banker of thirty-plus years, who is also my good friend and brother-in-law, Jim Forshey. Jim offered the sound advice of getting bad news to him quicker than good news, so he could help us through our problems. Thanks, Jim, for everything.

To my law firm and a couple of fellows named Chuck Emrick and Steve Kresnye, my profound thanks. And to our auditors, Tom Tracy, Mike Killeen, Larry Wolf, and Brian Gothot, for providing leading edge advice.

A most heartfelt and deep loving thanks to Bob Dorfmeyer, former President of Glidden Durkee Foods. In the darker moments of my business career, he accepted the Chairmanship of our newly-formed Advisory Board in 1982. Until his untimely passing, Bob was a guiding light, a mentor, and a great friend to me and my family.

To the Board of Advisors, the most talented people I have met in my travels, I offer thanks to you for the sage counsel that has kept the Manco Ducks flying high for all these years.

Thank you to all our vendors, without whom we would not exist. A very special thanks to Shuford Technologies, a partner for forty-plus years. The Shuford Family, Pope, sons Jim and Steve, along with great leaders like Glenn Hilton, Dave Taylor, Bill Little, Brad Dozier, and Steve Reese, became the model for all our dealings with other vendors. A handshake was the contract we operated on and it proved to be the best contract we could ask for. Special mention to Sealed Air Corporation and Leggett & Platt, invaluable partners in our vendor partnerships.

To all my partners, who are so much more than employees and who worked with me at Manco, Inc. (Henkel Consumer Adhesives), it is simply impossible to capture the size of my heart when I think of all of you. You contributed your heads, hearts, backs, and hands in service to our customers and one another. We formed a close family and learned to share the same giving spirit with our communities. To mention only a few is to slight too many. I will never forget you or your contributions to our team.

To our customers, you are the reason we come to work every day. You have been our boss, and a good one at that, for all these years. You collectively brought out the best in all of us. Wal-Mart and their speed challenged us the most. We responded and we are forever grateful for the opportunity. Our best customers in most cases were our best teachers and became our closest friends over time.

My thanks to my great motivators. To the great horse Secretariat: when I watched him win the Belmont to complete the Triple Crown in 1973, I said to myself, "From this day forward, I will become the best student and the best performer possible, regardless of comparing myself to others." From that moment on, I always looked to the finish line and didn't bother to look back to see who was running in second place.

To Jack Nicklaus, my contemporary, who thrilled me and motivated me and taught me that mental toughness, as well as talent and hard work, is what wins.

To Sam Walton, whom I was lucky to call a friend for sixteen years. Thanks, Sam, for teaching me that what my mother and father did around our kitchen table as I grew up was how you approached running your great Wal-Mart Company. You shared information, recognition, and rewards with everybody and you did it consistently. Once I learned that, business became simple. I knew from your example that I could build any size business as long as I remembered what I learned from my parents, as well as the great lessons I learned from you, Jack Shewmaker, Tom Coughlin, and so many others.

To my five beautiful children: John, Bill, Anne Marie, Julie, Lisa, and their respective husbands and wives, and my thirteen beautiful grandchildren who call me "Grandpa Jack," you continue to be my love and inspiration. Throughout my career, I've had the privilege of working daily at Manco, Inc. (Henkel Consumer Adhesives) with three of my children: John, who today is CEO; Bill, Executive Vice President Corporate Development; and Anne Marie Kahl, Director, Special Projects. My special thanks to their mother for the wonderful job she did of raising them when I was gone so much in the process of building the company.

To my friend of fifty years, Jack Kappus, who also built a successful business. Thanks for your advice, support, and friendship of a lifetime.

There would be no book without the special talents of Tom Donelan, a gifted writer and former Vice President of

Operations at Manco, Inc. Tom lived the Manco story with me for over ten years and with his great writing style, he was able to beautifully capture our story. Tom, I offer you my deep and heartfelt thanks for bringing our story to others.

To my right arm and special assistant, Christine Wright, who has been an invaluable help in keeping our Jack Kahl & Associates, LLC consulting business operating smoothly, and who has helped with the manuscript immensely. Christine, you did a considerable job in tightening this story for our readers.

To the twenty or so people who took the time to read the manuscript and provide advice, I offer my thanks for your insights and suggestions.

To Clint Greenleaf and his budding cast of stars like Nicole Hirsh, our editor, my thanks for guiding us through to completion on our first voyage into print.

Lastly, to the love of my life and best friend, Sherry, whose love and support for many years has brought joy and peaceful days to my life. You are my best friend and advisor.

-JKJ

• • •

Thanks to Jack for trusting me and for teaching me so much in my years at Manco. Still today, his lessons inspire me to lead from my heart. Thanks to my lovely wife, Ginny, for everything. Her patience with my demanding career and this writing addiction has always been remarkable. And thanks to my three children—Connor, Emily, and Brandon—for somehow teaching me what love really means, even when I thought I already knew.

-TJD

THE JOURNEY

If a man happens to find himself,
If he knows what he can be depended upon to do,
The limits of his courage,
The position from which he will no longer retreat,
The degree to which he can surrender his inner life to some
woman,
The secret reservoir of his determination,
The extent of his dedication,
The depth of his feeling for beauty,
His honesty and unpostured goals,
Then he has found a mansion which he can inhabit with dignity
all the days of his life.

– James Michener

The Choice to Lead

"It is high time the ideal of success should be replaced with the ideal of service."

Albert Einstein

What makes a great leader? The answer to that question is nothing less than the Holy Grail of the twenty-first century for leaders in business, politics, religion, sports, and the media alike. Thousands of books have been written on leadership already, and thousands more will follow. As the pace of our society quickens and the demand for real leadership grows, so does our need for knowledge that we can employ in our efforts to rise to the challenge.

From an academic view, leadership is a complex topic worthy of considerable discussion and debate. Leaders are forged in a cauldron of experience as the ores of personality, circumstance, and environment are melted, mixed, and fused. Leadership is a holistic property of personality, emerging from an immeasurable set of chaotic variables. Its birth is non-linear—it does not follow clean, predictable patterns.

As an entrepreneur and a leader, I appreciate the complex phenomenon of leadership; but I've made a career of simplifying the complex, and I think the same can be done for this topic. Despite the seemingly infinite set of ways in which leaders step forth, I think the essence of what they do is very simple.

Leadership is about achieving a goal through a team. To achieve a goal, a team needs help—help to gain resources and to remove obstacles. Leadership boils down to a *choice*—a choice to provide the *help* that the team needs in order to reach its goal. First and foremost, all leaders make that choice.

The choice to lead comes from an emotional commitment to the goal. No matter the degree of rational thought that developed the goal itself, in the end, the leader must emotionally believe that the goal is worth the effort, pain, and sacrifice such a journey requires. The leader must believe in the goal with his or her whole heart, for it is there, in the heart, where the choice to lead is made.

Jesus Christ said, "Many are called, but few are chosen." In the case of leadership we could say, *many are called, but few choose.* Many people study leadership, but too few dig deep inside themselves and make a choice to serve their team from the very heart of who they are. I hope this book will show you how important it is to do just that.

• • •

For nearly thirty years I was the owner and CEO of Manco, Inc., now Henkel Consumer Adhesives, North America. Over the course of my career I enjoyed good fortune and endured frightening challenges. I bought the tiny, industrial adhesive tape distributor in 1971, when its revenues were just $800,000. I was a poor kid from Cleveland's public housing neighborhood, selling insurance as my first job out of college; at the time, I was too scared to realize that just buying the company was an accomplishment in itself. When I retired from the company at the end of 2000, sales topped $300 million and those formative years as an industrial supplier were a distant memory. Our revenues came entirely from the consumer packaged goods arena, with adhesive tapes as the foundation of our success. Our talented team built the company around a wide variety of categories, including home weatherization products, mailing and shipping supplies, and kitchen and bath products such as shelfliners and bath mats.

Manco was (and, as part of Henkel, remains) a product sourcing, marketing, and distribution company with strong manufacturing partners behind it. Unencumbered by fixed investments, we were able to grow the company by listening to customers and reacting fluidly to the demands of an ever-changing market. We built partnerships with suppliers that excelled at manufacturing and product R&D, which allowed us to focus relentlessly on customer service. When we had money available to invest, we put it into strengthening our customer connections—our capital was in our people, not in machines. We hired the best and demanded the most. We rewarded success generously and forbade mediocrity. Listening to our customers and serving them with great care was Manco's competitive advantage, and it was our people who gave us the edge we needed.

Our flagship product became the Duck® brand of duct tape, which we introduced in the early 1980s. By the time I retired, Duck® Tape was the market leader, commanding more than 60 percent of the U.S. market. Duck® Tape is the ultimate household servant—it's the staple item in every toolbox. It can fix or extend the life of nearly anything you can imagine: rake handles, broomsticks, windowpanes, picture frames, model airplanes, dollhouses, you name it. We used to say Duck® Tape can "fix everything but a broken heart!" Duck® Tape is tough, tenacious, flexible, easy, fun—and it's not just a wonderful product, but a wonderful metaphor, too. It came to epitomize our corporate philosophy and culture. Duck® Tape held our world together.

Manco gained its foothold in consumer products in the late 1970s. We established a system of execution and built a strong base of business throughout the 1980s, ending the decade with revenues just over $50 million. We accelerated through the tumultuous 1990s, taking Manco as far as we could on our own. In 1998, we sold the company to a partner that brought the kind of resources and synergies that could maintain the growth of what had become a very large, global business.

Ours was truly a story of "David vs. Goliath." Our main competitor was 3M—a substantial and competent company with tremendous financial and human resources. 3M is a consumer products juggernaut—known for its innovative corporate culture and low-cost manufacturing excellence. While part of Manco's growth came from developing new products, new markets, and defeating other small companies, much of it came from chiseling market share away from 3M. Size didn't matter, but size of heart did. Our distinct advantage against 3M was the speed and passion of our people. We worked faster and harder than they did. Some might say we were more unconventional than our competition. Instead of management retreats and strategic planning meetings, our executives talked and planned in the hallways and bathrooms; instead of cautious, calculated secrecy, we shouted our intentions. Here and there we may have seemed smarter than 3M, but that was probably just luck. We learned to fix our mistakes faster; and our passion for success, coupled with fear for our survival, covered our deficiencies.

We lived like the gazelle in Aesop's fable, *The Lion and the Gazelle*, and wove the story into our own corporate mythology. The fable tells of a lion and a gazelle involved in a high-stakes game of survival. Each morning, the lion wakes up knowing he must run faster than the slowest gazelle in order *to eat* that day; meanwhile, a gazelle wakes up knowing she must run quicker than the fastest lion in order *to live*. Like the gazelle, we treated each and every day at Manco with the stakes of a life and death race.

Yet while our story is about a small company beating the odds, we learned our lessons from what is now the biggest company on Earth: Wal-Mart Stores, Inc. And what we learned was this: with the right values and the right culture, any team can beat any other team, regardless of size.

• • •

As a supplier to U.S. retail throughout the last quarter of the century, Manco had a front row seat to the transformation that reinvented our industry, redefined the American economy, and introduced *service* as the dominant component of our country's gross domestic product. Whether you call it the "Information Age," the "Post-Industrial Society," or any other age, there is no disputing that a new age has indeed dawned. I can't say that the tectonics of American retail or consumer goods supply ushered these changes upon the world, but I can say that the speed at which these changes affected our industry continues to astonish me. Information now displaces inventory. Intellectual capital supplants physical capital. Knowledge of the customer supersedes manufacturing power. Category management trumps product marketing. Store-focused merchandising has taken the place of top-level sales planning.

We navigated Manco through the landscape as it shifted with surreal speed. The age of information exploded onto the scene and globalization of production and supply became ubiquitous. Like a ship on the high seas, our only hope was to tack with the powerful winds of change. History will show that a perfect storm of economic force defined the 1990s, and our team was able to steer through it to reach port.

Our core strategies were simple; our tactics complex and ever changing. Ideas, products, and talent in our company evolved at a frenetic pace. In a world of such accelerated evolution there seems no suitable strategy, so ours became being fast, flexible, and passionate in order to *react to the moment*. We shot from the hip: we tried, failed, learned, and tried again. We found success in relentless persistence and late nights at the office; if we worked sixteen-hour days, the eight-to-ten-hours-a-day folks at 3M had to be *twice* as smart as us to win. Sure, we knew they had the resources and the financial advantage, but they couldn't be *that* much wiser than us. If we hired bright, energetic people and let them do their jobs, we could fight a successful guerrilla war and invent ways to succeed at every turn. Of course, the intensity of our fight wasn't for everyone we hired, but people who warmed to the demands of our business ultimately rose to the challenge of executive leadership.

Still, 3M—and the rest of our competitors—fought with brutal intensity. Our margins shrank and our focus on cost control bordered on religious zealotry. Our situation demanded creativity and spontaneity. We learned to be "tastefully poor" in our spending on facilities, benefits, and amenities so that our troops could be inspired by a decent lifestyle, while always remaining mindful of keeping costs low. Our chore was remarkably difficult, but what in life is easy? We cherished the challenge and were glad for the chance to be in the game.

We learned to let our customers define our priorities. To meet those demands, we installed a framework that ensured our ability to follow their lead profitably. Our R&D ideas came from the buyers' offices, not laboratories. We invented solutions that went far beyond the value of our products, and our retail partners appreciated that our egos were unhinged from blind allegiance to a product, brand, or manufacturing plant. We owed much of our flexibility to the fact that Manco was a distribution company, unencumbered by capital commitments in manufacturing. We made it our business to find the best manufacturing partners we could and leveraged their capabilities in production, as well as in research and development.

Product quality is a prerequisite. Part of our recipe for success was that we worked backward from what our retail customers and their consumers desired, rather than forward, from the viewpoint of tinkering with the way specific products were engineered. I learned to put quality first from the giant of retail himself, Sam Walton.

"Jack, do you know what a farmer does with duct tape?" he asked me in a Wal-Mart hallway one time.

"No, Mr. Walton, I don't," I said.

"He does *everything* with it." I recall how his eyes burned with that patented intensity, delivering the message imbedded in his words. "Promise me nothing but professional grade tape in my stores."

I nodded and said, "Yes."

"And never run out. But if you do run out, make sure it's our fault."

Sam explained that the entire image of his stores depended on a few key items. Duct tape was one of them. He could not afford to lose the loyalty of a customer over poor quality or a product shortage. Sam knew the customer was the boss. His number one job was to keep them happy.

With quality well established at the core of our product strategy, new marketing techniques took shape. Our packaging material improved to convince consumers that if the cover was good, the inside was good, too. Graphics and color marketing became synchronous across categories to improve communication of product features and benefits. Retailer product sets and well-executed promotions were designed to match the needs of specific consumer markets. In-store testing of new products—what we called "time trials"—came to supplement more traditional tools of consumer testing, as these trials offered both a practical and immediate view of what would sell, where it would sell, and why it would sell. Information drowned the landscape and we seized the power of those new currents; we learned to deliver region and store-specific programs that put our products right where they needed to be, with far less inventory and delivery expense than ever before.

Much of our success came from good fortune. Some might say that we were simply lucky—after all, we hitched our wagon to the right star. But luck is far more than serendipity; it is more than getting a break or good timing. Luck happens when you stay in the game. Luck happens when you're there when the break happens. Being in the right place at the right time has more to do with persistence than fate. And when lightening strikes, the opportunity must be recognized and seized. Execution is what turns blind luck into real fortune. As Terry Bowen, a good friend of mine and CEO of the Consumer Division of Leggett and Platt, an important supplier to Manco, has said, "Timing and dosage are everything." It's not just timing, but the *dosage* of *leadership* and *performance* that makes the difference.

So, here is where I take credit for the brilliance of our success, impressing you with stories of leadership genius and management miracles, right? Wrong! I'm proud to say that the first national story to chronicle our success was titled "Steal This Strategy," an article published in the February 1991 issue of *Inc. Magazine.* I make no bones about it: much of our success came from setting aside our egos in order to shamelessly steal ideas and adopt strategies that worked for the best organizations.

• • •

As some high-priced consultants call it, Manco aggressively "benchmarked" other companies, and adopted what we viewed as the best practices—except, we didn't follow a formal process or rigid framework for evaluating ideas, as those consultants would say you must. We just saw things that worked and tried them out. We called it "stealing shamelessly," and we learned the most from the greatest retailer that has ever existed. Wal-Mart is the brightest of all U.S. retail stars, and Sam Walton's leadership style as the founder and champion of that company inspired me as we fought our way through the competitive jungle.

Wal-Mart's operating system, however, stimulated our entire company and pushed our team as hard as I, or any of our other Manco leaders, could have. Wal-Mart demanded excellence from its business partners and we responded. In my final year of leading the team, Manco became the first company to ever receive *three* Wal-Mart "Vendor of the Year" awards in a single year. I could not have invented a more remarkable culmination to an exhilarating career.

Since I first met him, I have been an unabashed student of Mr. Sam, of the many leaders that continue his tradition of excellence, and of the remarkable culture that has fueled the greatest corporate triumph of the late twentieth century. I learned so much from this man that there is no way I could write a book on any topic—about business, life, or both—that's not anchored in the bedrock of his success. In fact, I even adopted the idea of "stealing shamelessly" from Mr. Sam. He and I exchanged dozens of letters through the years, but I'll never forget one in particular that shows his humility and willingness to learn from others. He writes about his team's ability to try ideas that they found at work elsewhere:

Dear Jack:

I don't know when I have received a letter I have appreciated more than the one you sent me. You always do so well in expressing yourself, your convictions, and your philosophy. I still contend you give me more credit than I deserve. Wal-Mart, as you well know, has taken a lot of pages out of a lot of people's books and so many of our associates—our management team as well as our folks in the stores—have made such wonderful contributions through the years . . . to have brought us to where we are. . . .

Sincerely,

Sam Walton

• • •

This book is simply a summary of what I've learned along the way—from Mr. Sam and many others whom I have either met personally or studied from a distance. It is a collection of other people's wisdom, stolen shamelessly. While there is no single leadership gene, no silver bullet, and alas, no Holy Grail, there is a collection of experiences that can be studied, understood, and applied. Every leader—no matter the gender, style, or temperament—can learn from other leaders and embrace common principles of success.

I have patched the words and ideas of many great leaders together to form a quilt of knowledge, with my own experience as the stitching. I have tried to simplify the complex into the essential personality traits that I believe define leaders: they must be *trustworthy*; they are lifelong *students*; they are *creative* and *driven* to succeed; they are *courageous* and *caring*; they are *disciplined*; and ultimately, they are *servants* to their team. To be sure, the expression of these traits varies as widely as the number of leaders out there doing their job today, but whatever the manifestation, these traits capture the essence of what it takes to lead. That said, there is still one more thing that is needed for leadership to rise. More than four hundred years ago, William Shakespeare wrote, "Some are born great, some achieve greatness, and some have greatness thrust upon 'em." His eloquence is indisputable, yet his definition is incomplete. No matter the greatness lurking inside a potential leader, nothing will come of it unless that person makes the choice to lead.

I'm proud to pass along the leadership lessons I have learned, but don't take my word for it. Eliminate the middleman and study the many references you'll find here. Charting your own path to discovery is where the adventure and the wisdom lives. As Johann Wolfgang Goethe said, "All truly wise thoughts have been thoughts already thousands of times; but to make them truly ours, we must think them over again honestly, till they take root in our personal experience."

Character Comes First

"Beyond rules, politics, strategy, and tactics, there is a basic philosophy of what is right."

From a sign posted at Manco

Ralph Waldo Emerson wrote, "Every great institution is the lengthened shadow of a single man." In other words, the character of the leader becomes the character of the organization. Through recruiting the right people and rewarding the right behaviors, a leader builds a team and creates an entity in his or her image. No trait of leadership is more important than the character that shapes the team.

Before a great team is built, however, the trust of the people who would join it must be earned. Of course, trust is the bedrock of any interpersonal relationship—why should it be any different when it comes to the relationships between leaders and their teams? Trust engages the heart of the follower and this is what encourages people to give their emotional commitment to a cause. When teammates trust one another they fling themselves into their work, bringing emotions like passion, pride, love, and even anger to the table. Without full and complete trust, a leader can only win a kind of cold, mercenary-like allegiance to his or her vision. And as most know, the degree of a team's emotional commitment is often what separates otherwise equally talented competitors.

In a 1988 *Wall Street Journal* essay, Peter Drucker effectively boiled leadership down to trust for the same reason: "The
final requirement of effective leadership is to earn trust.
Otherwise there won't be any followers—and the only definition
of a leader is someone who has followers."

As a supplier to Wal-Mart, I chose to follow Sam Walton's
lead; I devoted my company to helping Wal-Mart succeed
because he earned my trust. Of course, before I met him, I knew
Sam was a supreme merchant. His competence at retailing had
already earned my respect, but this respect became a very
personal trust as I got to know him. Sam was a good, honest,
fair man, but strong moral character was only part of why I
trusted him as a leader. Much of it came from his entire system
of personal values—values such as responsibility, work ethic,
and thrift—which I not only saw in him, but also mirrored by
his company. A servant leader like Mr. Sam succeeds because he
earns the trust of his team through three crucial elements of
character: competence, moral values, and shared, personal
values of performance.

COMPETENCE

A leader must have the knowledge to lead. Without the relevant
knowledge or skills, decisions are not credible. If a leader has
competence, those following him or her will trust that he or she
understands the situations the organization faces. The team will
trust that their leader knows best. They will forgive the occa-
sional mistake and lapse in judgment because they know that the
best effort was made, and is always made, to solve problems and
fix mistakes. After character, the next most critical trait of leadership is being a lifelong student. We will discuss the importance

of seeing yourself as a student of the world in the next chapter, but for now, keep in mind that knowledge and credibility are key to earning the respect and trust of others.

MORAL VALUES

People form an emotional bond with leaders who act within similar moral frameworks. Like attracts like. People trust others when they can rely upon them to make the same moral decisions that they themselves would make if they were leading the team. So much of moral character boils down to honesty. Unfortunately, my experience has shown me that people who have trouble being honest don't just lack character, but are usually covering up other fatal flaws. Flaws of competence or arrogance, for example.

Of course, leadership does require some degree of discretion with the facts—the need for secrecy surrounding a key strategic project, for instance, may dictate that the facts be kept vague, or withheld altogether. But there is a difference between the "white lies" that may be necessary to maintain the team's focus, compared to dishonesty regarding the routine execution of the team. Any outright dishonesty by a leader will eventually be exposed and trust will quickly be washed away.

None of this is to say that bonds of trust are forged only between those of *sound* moral character. I wish it were so, but history is replete with examples of immoral and downright evil leaders. Evidently, those leaders earned the trust of equally immoral followers. The point is, people will follow a leader who earns their trust by acting in ways that they feel are important to success—whether or not their definition of success is for good or not.

Tom Coughlin, my good friend and CEO of Wal-Mart's Stores Division, once described a speech about leadership he heard General Norman Schwartzkopf deliver. Schwartzkopf began his remarks by asking the audience to take notes. When he saw only a few folks make the effort to prepare paper and pen, he shouted, "I said to take notes!" As you might imagine, the crowd snapped to attention and obliged.

While the audience paid close attention and took copious notes, Schwartzkopf went on to describe twelve of his fourteen "rules of leadership." After rule twelve, Schwartzkopf stopped abruptly and told the audience that he hadn't told them anything that they did not already know. He said that the only two rules that meant anything were the final two he was about to give them: rules thirteen and fourteen.

In an abrupt change of command, Schwartzkopf directed the group to tear up the notes they had so diligently compiled. The confused audience looked at Schwartzkopf and at their handwritten pages. Either frozen by the "about face" of orders, or reluctant to scrap a lot of hard work, the audience did nothing. Stormin' Norman shouted, "I said throw out your notes!" The crowd seemed to jerk forward in a unified, spastic motion. Notes were crumpled, torn, and otherwise destroyed in a matter of moments. As the melee ended, Schwartzkopf calmly outlined the lesson that he wanted his students to learn:

Rule thirteen: When given command, take command.

Rule fourteen: If you don't know what to do, do what is right.

Think about that. Rule thirteen says a lot of things: it says something about initiative, it says something about courage, and it says something about knowledge and credibility. It has to do with trust because it has to do with the credibility of taking command, acting like a leader, and seizing the respect of your team.

But rule fourteen is emphatically rooted in moral values: *when in doubt, do what you think is right.* I love the way Schwartzkopf drove his point home, but I have to say that I already knew rule fourteen. In fact, I learned rule fourteen from my parents years ago.

The fact is, character is forged at home. The moral values of a family, however big or small and whatever its composition, are the values of the future leader. Whatever my mother and father modeled into the clay of my soul became my idea of what is right. I cannot tell you how many times I sat alone with the burden of great responsibility and reached for nothing more than my instincts to make a decision. I thank God (and my folks) that those instincts were grounded in the right values. In fact, we posted a sign at Manco with the quotation that introduces this chapter to remind ourselves that in a world saturated with data, character is sometimes all you have when making a tough choice.

PERSONAL PERFORMANCE VALUES

Character is defined by a broad system of values—not all of which can be clearly understood in the moral terms of right and wrong. When we consider the character of a person, or a company, we must not only consider the obvious moral ethics, but also many other elements that comprise the complete, personal value system of the person or organization. These values include responsibility, work ethic, thrift, and fairness.

Like moral values, these are forged at home.

When I was about seven years old, our family lived in one of Cleveland's low-income public housing neighborhoods. My father became ill with tuberculosis and was admitted to the hospital, where he stayed for many months. Money was as tight as ever without Dad working. My mom brought all of us kids together—I was the oldest son of a family that would grow to total six children—and said that we each had to work as a team to keep the family afloat.

"Jack," she said to me, "You're the man of the house until Dad comes home." I was struck with feelings of pride, responsibility, and fear all at once.

A few weeks later, I was outside sledding when she came out and asked me to get a job. Later that day, more than a little scared, but determined to do my duty for her and our family, I approached the neighborhood *Cleveland News* driver as he made a stop near our house. At the time, *The News* was Cleveland's afternoon newspaper.

"Hey, mister," I said, "I need a job."

"How old are you?" he asked.

"Seven."

"Why do you need a job?"

"My daddy's in the hospital."

Although I was young, I could see a mix of respect and pity in his eyes. "I have carriers for all of my routes," he said, "but if you can get yourself any new customers, you can make your own route."

I called on every apartment in the neighborhood and found one customer: an old lady who probably felt sorry for me. I found another customer down the hill and near the river in a bar called The Harbor Inn—a Cleveland landmark, which, back in the day, served sailors from around the world.

The Harbor Inn was always my favorite customer. I remember being hoisted to a seat of honor atop the bar, buying a Pepsi (in those days, a nickel bought a bit more Pepsi than Coke), and listening to the voices of the world talk treason, politics, religion, sex . . . all the topics that will set a seven-year-old mind adrift! I quickly learned that if I took good care of this customer, they would take care of me—whether by just welcoming me to sit a while, or by giving me a "tip" with a free soda. Within a few months, a kid quit his route and I picked up five of his customers. Soon, another quit and I picked up his customers, too. By the time I was ten years old, I had twenty-two customers. When we moved out of public housing and into a working class suburb, I got a route with seventy-six customers.

My siblings and I saved our money in our own bank accounts until my mom asked us to use the money to buy something the family needed. I bubbled with pride when we earned enough to buy a new garage door. It was hard work and a lot of pressure for a kid, but the feeling of joy and satisfaction that came from helping my family was simply unforgettable. People depended upon me and I helped them. My responsibility to my family made me feel great! From those childhood experiences, responsibility became imbedded in my system of values. As a leader at Manco, I became surrounded by people who shared such beliefs. I either found them and brought them onto the team, or they came to the team and learned that responsibility was a value I expected them to embrace. Like attracts like.

Thomas Edison's words ring so true: "Genius is 1 percent inspiration and 99 percent perspiration." Success is seldom found in bold strokes of genius, serendipity, or great fortune. Each of us loves to hear those dramatic stories, but the fact is that most successful people earn their stripes through hard work and brute force. Perspiration is doubly demanded of the leader;

leaders are always asked to give more time than they have available. But don't overlook the fact that a leader's *work ethic* radiates throughout the team, setting the tone for the entire organization's performance.

If my mother's dedicated efforts to raise a big family through some lean times taught me lessons of responsibility, it is only fair to say that my father, who worked two jobs for many years, set a great example of work ethic. On top of his personal example, he taught me a great deal through his uncompromising expectations. He was tough, especially on the three boys in our family. He demanded hard work from us, and he wouldn't tolerate laziness or irresponsibility.

Many years later, when he was in his seventy-fourth year, he tearfully told me why he held us to such seemingly rigid standards. My dad grew up in poverty, yet managed to excel in school. He did so well in his studies that he was able to skip the fourth grade. A year later, he begged his teachers to let him stay in the sixth grade, and not skip into the seventh, so that he could stay close to his friends. He earned a full scholarship to the most prominent Catholic high school in Cleveland at the time, Cathedral Latin. But Cathedral Latin was a long way from where my dad's family lived.

The commute was tough, but the social gap between my father's neighborhood and the neighborhoods the other kids at that school called home was even greater. On top of that, he was the smallest, youngest kid in his class. He did what most little boys would do to earn the respect of his peers, and took on the role of the fearless prankster. In fact, he became such a little terror, he ultimately got himself kicked out of the school.

Ever since then, there hasn't been a day in his life when he didn't regret that choice. He resolved to mold his kids with the discipline to work hard, as it was a discipline that he felt he had lacked. And at that he certainly succeeded. I'll never claim to be the smartest consumer products strategist in the world, but I sure know the value of hard work. In fact, I attribute Manco's first entrance into Wal-Mart as the result of nothing more than hard work.

The year was 1976, and I was sitting in my small ten-by-ten foot booth at the 1976 National Home Center Show—the first one ever held. It was about thirty minutes before the show was scheduled to end, and the big hall was settling down. Some of my neighbors had already packed their booths and left to get a jump on their travels home; others had begun to tear down their displays. As I sat there alone, I gritted my teeth and looked at my watch. I told myself that I had to run through the tape at the end of the race.

A short time later, a man came into my booth and introduced himself as Gary Broach, a buyer from Wal-Mart. He said he had another meeting to attend, but would like to talk with me about our home insulation products. He asked if I could wait for him.

I waited for Gary for an hour or two. By the time he came back, the hall was dark and empty. We talked about Manco's products for a while. Ultimately, he ended up writing me the biggest order in Manco's short history: it totaled $88,000. I'd stayed so late that I'd missed my plane, but when Gary apologized for keeping me from my family, I told him, "Don't worry about it. I think I could fly home without a plane right now!"

Who knows? Maybe our products were better than the competitor's up the aisle—but he had packed up his things and left by mid-day. Maybe I was just "lucky" to have stuck it out.

H. Ross Perot said, "Success breeds arrogance and complacency. Average people always beat the best and brightest." We hung that sign on our wall at Manco to remind us that shoe leather beats intellectual theory *every* time. You can be the smartest and most creative person the world has ever seen, but if you don't have the work ethic to match that distinct talent, you won't get very far. As Thomas Edison put it, "An idea is something that won't work unless you do."

By now, it should be clear that my family was always trying to wring more from a dollar; unsurprisingly, thrift was another value I learned in my early years. It's a safe bet that Sam Walton learned how much hard-working folks appreciated the value of a dollar during his childhood, too. He not only grew up during the Great Depression, but he grew up in Oklahoma—a time and place immortalized for its stark, dustbowl despair in Steinbeck's *The Grapes of Wrath*.

While Sam's family held tight and supported themselves, he was witness to the poverty and failure of his many neighbors. I'm quite certain that Mr. Sam learned the value of keeping costs low and passing the savings along to his customers from those tough, early days. I'm equally certain that his experience forged a character determined to share good fortune with others—a value which both the early Wal-Mart associates and current associates alike would surely attest to today.

THE VALUES AMPLIFIER

The rash of recent financial crises at major U.S. corporations is a crisis of ethical leadership. Leaders create the value system of their organizations. They recruit and develop teammates whose values are like theirs. They set policies that reflect their own standards of conduct. Perhaps most importantly, they make decisions that ripple throughout their team. Each and every decision becomes part of the fabric of that team, part of the value system of that company. Jack Shewmaker, Director of Wal-Mart Stores, Inc., and a good friend of mine, recently wrote to former Vice President Walter Mondale:

> *In a corporation . . . the ethical standards are largely defined by the leadership. In many cases, it is an ongoing review of events and responses which results in a reiteration of the corporation's values. Leadership guides those events and responses, and sets the moral tone of the team.*

Shewmaker was Wal-Mart's President from 1978 to 1988—arguably the inflection point in the growth that positioned them to become the powerhouse they are today. Currently, he chairs two of Wal-Mart's Board committees: strategy and finance. He knows a thing or two about the ethical standards it takes to build a business. As Wal-Mart's President, he knew that the company's merchandise buyers made decisions worth countless dollars of profit to its vendors and hopeful vendors. He knew that some vendors might stop at nothing to influence a buyer's judgment, so he and Wal-Mart established the retail industry's strictest corporate gift policy and management statement. Shewmaker drew a tight line on defining a gift; he wanted to ensure that his buyers remained devoutly objective to the needs of Wal-Mart's customers, not subject to the influence of deep pockets or special friends.

A leader has to "walk the talk" of core values. The entire team is watching and taking cues from the leader regarding acceptable actions and behaviors. If a leader chooses a path of dishonesty in any way, the organization will take notice. His behavior will be mirrored by those he is trying to lead; it will surge through the ranks because people will naturally assume that what's good for the goose, is good for the gander as well. People will adopt the example of behavior they are given— whether those examples are communicated directly or not—and in this way, a leader's actions are amplified throughout the organization. One brutal reality of life is that we are all human, and human moral behavior is imperfect. Even the most ethical leaders will face crises and challenges that cloud their judgment. Leaders can find themselves caught up in the magnitude of a tough situation and try to rationalize "extenuating circum- stances" or "contributing factors," and in the process, hide the ethical perspective from their own view. Or, they might try to justify a slight, immoral decision as sensible; given the enormous consequences of failure, they tell themselves a small breech of ethics is okay. But it is not. Whether they mask the ethical dilemma from their own view, or claim that the end justifies the means, these leaders need help. They need the strength of their organization to come to their aid. They need their closest friends and confidants—or even just a colleague caught in the cross- fire—to step up and remind them of the rules of the game. In a harsh and unforgiving world, character is often a team effort. We need to remember that the "easy way out" can only haunt us in the end. Any ethical breech, however great, small, or seem- ingly justifiable, is still an ethical breech.

SHOW TRUST TO EARN TRUST

At the start of this chapter, I said that leadership is built upon a relationship between a leader and a follower. While a leader may prove to have the competence and the character to be considered trustworthy by others, he or she will not necessarily build a rela- tionship that earns their trust. Only by respecting the value of others and trusting them, can a person earn the trust of others. *Only by giving, do you receive.*

But there is a big caveat to this rule: you can't give away something that you don't have. A leader must trust himself before trusting others, and surely before he expects others to trust him in return.

Trust extends beyond your own corporation's walls, however. I recall being in more than a few meetings at Wal-Mart where various executives and leaders talked about the power of their information systems and the enormous amount of data the company collects regarding point-of-sale transactions, product logistics, and so on. By the end of the last millennium, the amount of data stored by Wal-Mart exceeded even that of the U.S. government. What is so wonderful, though, is that Wal-Mart liberally makes this data available to suppliers so they can analyze their business with the retailer and drive improvements. This is telling; instead of choosing to hoard such valuable resources, this gigantic company decided to *trust* suppliers to improve business. Many suppliers looked upon this tactic with skepticism; they assumed that Wal-Mart was simply pushing responsibilities and costs onto them. This attitude may have become a self-fulfilling prophecy for many of these suppliers, as they did nothing with Wal-Mart's mandate to make their companies better. Meanwhile, the smarter suppliers used the data to expand sales and decrease their costs. They seized on the opportunity to improve their own performance. These wise companies viewed Wal-Mart's move as one of partnership and trust, and they returned the favor. Once they knew that Wal-Mart trusted their intelligence and commitment to succeed, they began to trust Wal-Mart to help them implement changes that would inevitably benefit everyone: supplier, retailer, and consumer alike.

If you guessed that Wal-Mart's philosophy of sharing information sprang from Mr. Sam's values, you guessed right. One of Sam's Ten Rules for Building a Business states, "Communicate everything you possibly can to your partners. The more they know, the more they'll understand. The more they understand, the more they'll care. If you don't trust your associates to know what's going on, they'll know you don't really consider them partners."

You must realize and accept that you can't know everything, nor will you be prepared for every situation you come across, but you can always choose to do the right thing. In the end, the world revolves around relationships between people, and trust is at the heart of all human relationships. Whenever ego or greed threatens to get in the way of your value system, remember the words of Charles F. Banning:

> *If all the gold in the world were melted down into a solid cube, it would be about the size of an eight-room house. If a man got possession of all that gold . . . billions of dollars worth . . . he could not buy a friend, character, peace of mind, clear conscience, or a sense of eternity.*

Banning's words are a great way to say something very simple: *Do the right thing.*

A Lifetime of Learning

"Leadership and learning are indispensable to each other."

John F. Kennedy

The best definition of a leader I have ever heard comes from Capt. Michael McKean, former head of leadership training for the U.S. Army, based at the Pentagon. His decades of teaching leadership skills led him to say, "A leader has all the qualities of a child—an insatiable curiosity for learning, a boundless energy to put the learning into practice, and an ability to adapt to new behaviors very quickly."

Note where McKean begins: *an insatiable curiosity for learning.* Successful leadership is not possible without a complete commitment to learning. The aspiring leader must have an unquenchable thirst for knowledge—whether it is thirst for knowledge about a product, service, customer, competitor, an industry, colleague, process, or technology; whether it is about business, war, science, people or art, you simply cannot lead people to success without the competence that springs from knowledge.

KNOW WHAT YOU DON'T KNOW

The basis of all macro and micro economic systems is the effort to utilize scarce resources to serve unlimited demands. The goal of the leader is to navigate his or her organization through the heart of that fundamental equation. The art of choosing the right priorities from those unlimited demands is the thing that determines success or failure. How can the right choices be made without knowledge of the environment? The situation? The people on the team?

The effective leader is a student who yearns for knowledge of his or her world. There is no room to waste in the mind of a leader. That mind must be sharpened by study, so that intelligent decisions—or at least educated guesses—can be made and the odds of success increased. Napoleon said, "Nothing is more difficult, and therefore more precious, than to be able to decide." If deciding is so important, then the preparation—the learning—that precedes a decision must be even more so.

As with many lessons, my mother taught me how important it was to first know and understand a situation before making a decision. Each Saturday she would take my younger brother Jimmy and me down to Cleveland's West Side Market to buy groceries. I always loved going to the Market—the hustle of a busy Saturday and the free trade of meat and produce electrified me. Typically we went late in the day, when the vendors were discounting their goods to move unsold inventory. The ripest produce carried the sharpest price and was often sold in the alley behind the stand; if it went unsold, it would spoil before the next market day. One time, my mother picked up some tomatoes from the off-counter basket of a produce vendor—she was planning to stew and jar them. Knowing the tomatoes were cheap, my brother and I figured we were helping her when we loaded our arms with as many tomatoes as we could carry. My mother turned to us and said, "Jack, leave the rest. I only have two hands and so many Mason jars—I don't want to waste any. *A bargain isn't a bargain unless you need it.*"

I learned something then that I have never forgot, though I could not describe the lesson until I was much older. "Unless you *need* it," she said. You must understand the *needs* and demands of your environment—your context—in order to make effective decisions. Finding a great opportunity only brings good fortune if you know how it suits your situation. Over the course of my life, I have learned that I must always study and understand the world in which I live, relentlessly seeking to ensure that my objectives fit their contexts.

Tom Coughlin of Wal-Mart recalls his own humbling lesson about the importance of learning. One day Tom joined Sam and Bud Walton—Sam's brother and Wal-Mart's co-founder—as they flew out to Texas from their office in northwestern Arkansas to visit a Wal-Mart store that was about to open. After visiting the store, the three men drove across town to their chief local competitor, a Gibson's store. To Tom's eye, the store was dirty and unkempt. As they left to return home, Bud Walton turned to Tom and asked him what he'd seen at Gibson's. Tom proudly and effortlessly rattled off the long list of shortcomings he'd noticed: the windows were dirty, merchandising was sloppy, stock was thin, the checkout line was long and unmanaged, and on and on and on. He finished with a smug smile.

Bud nodded, turned to Sam, and asked what he had seen. Looking out the car window as they left the lot, Sam replied reflectively with his own list—but his list was about what he had seen Gibson's doing *right*. Sam noticed a great deal on pillows, two for five dollars. He saw bed sheets with 10 percent more thread count than Wal-Mart's for the same price. He met a hardware department salesman who knew his business *and* his customers. Sam went on and on and on, and Tom's six-foot, four-inch frame sank deep into the rear car seat until he felt about three-feet tall.

Tom told me later, "I learned a lesson from Mr. Sam that day that I never forgot. You can learn something anywhere. No matter how much better than your competitors you *think* you are, there is always *something* they do better than you. Find it." By following Mr. Sam's example of leading by learning, Wal-Mart has dominated the retail landscape for the past decade.

Like Tom, I have learned from a lifetime of humbling experiences. What I have come to see is that learning springs from a deep humility and a willingness to admit that you simply do not know it all. Learning begins with a mind that is prepared to accept new knowledge. An arrogant mind that excludes new ideas is doomed to fail. The leader must adopt the philosophical attitude espoused by Socrates, who said, "One thing only I know, and that is that I know nothing." I felt so strongly about the importance of humility as the key to learning that I hung a sign with Socrates' words above my office door at Manco.

There is another reason I embrace the wisdom of Socrates' statement so fervently. Early in Manco's history we had a run of several successful years. Our team was growing fast—in the span of a decade, we'd grown from revenues of under $1 million to over $30 million, and had hired several dozen new people. We started to think we were something special, when suddenly, we found ourselves facing a serious financial crisis. Our financial officer fell way behind on his work, impacting everything from paying accounts on time to properly reporting the company's cash flow and profitability. The discovery hit us like a runaway freight train—suddenly, I found myself staring straight into the awful abyss of financial ruin. It was then that I knew that we weren't something so special at all, but that we needed help.

From the ashes of near disaster we built a new and better

team, and our company became stronger for it. But I went further: I took the steps to create an advisory board and sought the counsel of some key Cleveland professionals. It wasn't a governing board of the company, per se, but a group of experts who believed in our potential and committed some of their time toward helping us succeed. My goal was to surround myself with sharp, experienced people who could teach and coach our key executives and me. That board became the rudder that steered our ship. I simply cannot overstate how important their guidance and advice was and continues to be.

I'll never forget the moment when I approached Bob Dorfmeyer, a successful executive at a Cleveland consumer products company, and asked him if he'd like to lead this new group. He said, "Jack, I wouldn't like to—I'd *love* to." Bob remained my friend and mentor until he died several years ago. He always told me that his number one job was to teach Jack Kahl to believe in himself. My self-styled system of building my self-confidence involved a tireless effort to learn from books, trade shows, customers, colleagues, and advisors.

In a world literally flooded with information, the effective leader needs to be a sponge. The leader must learn fast in order to remain credible as an expert in the eyes of his or her team. But there is an important paradox to understand: there are limits to what we can know. The best leaders will find that they cannot know everything; they must be able to let go of their ego—not merely in order to learn new things, but also to recognize what they *cannot* learn. They need to know when they should trust their team's ability to accomplish what they cannot.

LEARN FROM THE PEOPLE WHO KNOW

Two decades ago, when Sam Walton wrote down his Ten Rules for Building a Business, he advised: "Listen to everyone in your company ... they are the only ones who really know what's going on out there. You'd better find out what they know." Sam realized that the people on the front lines knew more than managers and executives could know from their seats behind their desks. He knew that the effective leader had to be out in the field, listening and asking questions. That is how true knowledge about the business is gained.

Mr. Sam's philosophy echoes the advice of great military leaders. General Colin Powell has a leadership rule that says, "The commander in the field is always right, and the rear echelon is wrong, unless proved otherwise." Powell probably learned a thing or two from his study of General George Patton. Patton often personally visited his troops on the front lines, learning firsthand from their perspective and experience. Patton said to his officers, "I want every member of this staff to get up front at least once every day. You will never know what is going on unless you can hear the whistle of the bullets." By sharing their vulnerability, Patton humanized his role as a leader, earned the respect and trust of his men, and surely fueled their inspiration. So if you want to retain a pompous, self-important viewpoint, stay in your office and limit your exposure to reality. But, if you want to learn, go where the knowledge is. Listen to your people and work alongside them.

Speaking of the front lines, here is one piece of advice that I know can help any aspiring leader. When you attend a speech or a seminar of any sort, sit in the front row. I'm always amazed at how many people spend their company's money to learn something, but sit in the back of the room doodling or slipping out to check their voicemail. Few people ever try to sit near the speaker. Nothing forces your attention more than sitting up front, devoting all of your attention to what a speaker has to say, and thus, opening yourself up completely to new learning. I remember jumping over cordons and running through aisles to get a front row seat, always wondering why so many people were scurrying to find a chair in a corner of the room. What were they there for?

Sam Walton managed to learn from anyone, anywhere, anytime. He knew his associates had plenty of knowledge to share, but he also knew that everyone he met could enrich his life somehow. I remember a brief, personal exchange with Sam that humbled me and changed my life.

I was visiting Wal-Mart, waiting in their lobby with another Manco executive early one morning. While executives at Wal-Mart could use a hallway that routed them around the lobby, Mr. Sam always preferred to walk through the reception area, taking the opportunity to speak with vendors and other guests who happened to be waiting for appointments. Though I'd just met him once before, Sam recognized me as he made his way from the executive area to the merchandising offices, and he came over to say hello.

Shifting his stack of reading papers from a night of home-work, he said, "Hi guys, how's business out there?"

"Pretty good," I said. "We're glad to be selling Wal-Mart." My voice quivered—I couldn't stop myself from being nervous around the man.

He looked at me closely. "You're Jack, aren't you?"

"Yes," I said. "Nice to see you, Mr. Sam."

We talked for a few moments about Wal-Mart's recent sales performance and the economy. I made a few comments about Wal-Mart's unique culture and its growing success—admittedly with a bit of brown-nosing! Sam's sharp eyes burned as if they were doing the listening.

"Jack," he said, "You're a real student of management, aren't you?"

"I try to be," I said. "I have a lot to learn."

"So do I. Jack, if you'll share what you're reading with me, I'll be glad to learn from you and share back whatever I know."

I nearly fell to the floor! What could I possibly teach this great entrepreneur? Back home in my office, I almost chickened out. I questioned Sam's sincerity; I questioned my own ability to articulate worthwhile ideas to him; I questioned the risk of giving him something that he didn't like. In the end, I didn't chicken out. I had an invitation to begin a close relationship with a blossoming, retail juggernaut, and I convinced myself to accept it. Mr. Sam opened to me, and I opened back. I know I learned plenty from him. I only hope that I returned at least a fraction of the favor.

TEACHING IS LEARNING

Even the effort to teach is grounded in the effort to learn. Ralph Waldo Emerson said it well: "It is one of the most beautiful compensations of this life that no man can try to sincerely help another without helping himself." If a leader is defined as someone responsible for helping others achieve a goal, then a leader is someone who is always learning from that process.

Wal-Mart's famous Saturday morning meetings follow the very same idea of learning by teaching. Each week executives and managers convene to culminate a busy week of bee-hiving across the country. Their purpose is to share information and elevate the collective knowledge of the team. They tell stories and have fun, but they also look hard at the numbers and challenge themselves to improve the business. By sharing the knowledge they've learned while out in the field, everybody on the team learns, and everybody leaves the meeting as an entrepreneur empowered to make decisions. To borrow Emerson's phrase, the "beautiful compensation" of this integral process is that the effort of sharing information requires the speakers to refine their thoughts, effectively helping them to study and reinforce what they have learned.

We adopted the same formula of holding boundaryless, information-sharing meetings at Manco and it made a tremendous contribution to our success. Everyone was welcome to this agenda-free session. Like a good jazz band, we played off of our own energy and improvised our way through experiences. We shared stories from the road—trade shows, customer visits, supplier audits—and we talked about progress on product development and technology projects. By ensuring that knowledge was transferred and experience was gained collectively, our Thursday meetings cemented a culture of information sharing, trust, and employee empowerment, which helped us craft a common vision of success. Then, like a football team breaking the huddle, everyone came out of that meeting knowing the play, and we moved the ball steadily downfield against 3M.

For years, we operated the company through only that meeting. When sales reached $100 million, we added an operations meeting for key managers, directors, and vice-presidents. We kicked off each Monday morning with a review of critical performance measures and created the needed actions and reactions to guide the business. Eventually, we stopped holding our executive meetings in the hallways and created a third, weekly session for our top managers to get together to talk about strategy. So, on three days of every week, our executive team started the day at 7:30 a.m., always working together, though with different participants, refining the rhythm that comes from teamwork—the rhythm any jazz band leader knows is so important to great music.

Creative Vision

"Some men see things as they are and say, 'Why?' I dream of things that never were and say, 'Why not?'"

George Bernard Shaw

"An insatiable curiosity for learning . . . " That is how Capt. Michael McKean's definition of leadership begins. *Curiosity* implies a mind eager to learn. But the curious mind is also a creative mind; it considers a realm of possibilities that other minds never imagine. The creative mind is driven to throw light against the darkness of ignorance and advance down the uncertain path of discovery.

Curiosity is the basis for creativity—it is the driving force that gives the mind the desire to wander. Every mind is creative to some extent, every mind is curious and driven to discover, but creativity manifests in so many different ways. Creativity can be revealed in one person through bold images—drawings, sketches, and the like. In another, through powerfully eloquent words; and yet another, through a spreadsheet that makes statistical figures dance to the tune of important business strategies.

Creativity is not just about *stylistic appearances*. We are often quick to call a graphic designer a "creative" person, but we do not use the same label for a financial manager or an engineer. Yet, who would deny that creativity lies at the heart of all great work and problem solving? We can readily distinguish between artistic and mechanistic thinkers, but why don't we see the artist and the mechanist as equally creative problem solvers? If our definition of creativity is limited to artistic expressions, we are missing the bigger picture of creative potential that exists in all people, at all levels on a team.

Creative thinking is the engine of entrepreneurship and has a well-deserved place in the business landscape. Moreover, creativity influences leadership in many diverse, yet interrelated ways. I want to spend some time teasing apart the wonderful web of creativity that affects leadership. But first I must offer the following disclaimer: sometimes a rose is just a rose. Hopefully my effort to segment creativity into its parts does not destroy the essence of what it really is.

CRAFTING A VISION

The creative mind is childlike—unashamed to dream, tinker, or fantasize. Black Elk, a wise, twentieth-century Native American, embraced this idea when he said, "Grown men can learn from very little children, for the hearts of children are pure . . . the Great Spirit may show to them many things which older people miss." A leader instinctually finds a way to stave the inevitable transition into ritualized adulthood. The leader finds a way to keep some of that childish purity and dares to dream as others settle for the vanilla world of conformity surrounding them.

When we built the current corporate headquarters for Manco, we renamed the street hosting the building to *Just Imagine Drive*. We wanted our *partners*, which is what employees and executives alike were called at Manco, to be bombarded with the idea of using their imagination *everywhere*: on the street as they drove to and from work, on their business

cards, on their letterhead. It's too easy to succumb to the machi-
nations of life and work, and forsake the creative mind with
which we are all endowed.

The leader's mind imagines a future unseen by others. A
vision takes shape as the leader considers the current world,
evaluates trends, sifts through information, and begins to formu-
late ideas for a new tomorrow. There is seldom a moment of
divine inspiration or the cry of "eureka!" The process of envi-
sioning the future is not a mysterious gift: it is simply a well-
developed form of pattern recognition common to the human
brain. But in the mind of a leader, the routine of recognizing
opportunities extends into a horizon too cloudy for most to see.
The leader's vision is never perfect; in fact, you might liken it to
the way a sculptor approaches a block of stone. Creative ideas
move the artist to begin, but the vision changes as the rock
reveals its strengths and soft spots, and as the artist reacts to the
developing work.

FOSTERING INNOVATION

We hung a sign at Manco that read: "Bring ideas in and entertain them royally, for one of them may be king." We always kept
our eyes and minds wide open for great ideas. Vision is a must
for any leader, but in the end, it has to be a vision that creates
value for the customer. The only reason a business exists is to
serve customers in a profitable manner. In the long run, innovation is the only thing that sets a company apart from its competitors and earns the respect and loyalty of its customers. Typically,
innovation is understood in terms of product development or
marketing—but not always, maybe not even most of the time.

Again, consider Wal-Mart: the company has innovated as

much in the worlds of technology and logistics as it has in the world of merchandising. In fact, Lee Scott, Wal-Mart's CEO, rose through the company's distribution and logistics ranks to take the top job. Lee's career says a lot about the kind of thinking that drives the biggest company on the planet. Innovative operating techniques, which create and accelerate efficiency, are what make Wal-Mart a success.

Manco adopted a customer-centric approach to innovation, adjusting its business model to serve specific customers in specific ways, rather than walking the well-trodden path of product focus. To us, relationships, not the products we sold, were the key. We could have been selling flypaper instead of duct tape—our innovation came from listening to our customers and reacting to their needs. Because we were not hung up on the products we made or sold, we were able to look at our retail partners' businesses through their eyes. Their eyes were on entire categories of products, not just the products themselves. Their eyes were on their stores and how they served different communities of customers. Their eyes were on reducing their inventory levels through variables, such as carton package quantity and replenishment algorithms. We invested in sales teams and gave their leaders a supporting cast of marketing, financial, and analytical teammates, along with the right technological tools, and told them to work together to understand everything about their customers' businesses. We used that same relationship-based mentality with our product sourcing approach. We felt that trust was the crucial ingredient for success. Trust bred speed, and speed bred responsiveness to our customers. We forged alliances and partnerships with the best industrial manufacturers, effectively becoming their distribution partner into retail. For a time, everything was done on a handshake—we never had a contract. We were loath to let lawyers get in the way of a relationship and hamper our flexibility to react to the market and do the right thing. We never wanted to stifle the kind of innovation that drove our business. We wanted to maximize our ability to entertain many potential "kings."

Our biggest and best partnership was with Shurtape Technologies, Inc., the manufacturer of our duct and masking tape. In all the years I owned Manco, we never had a written contract with Shurtape, despite the fact that our purchases from them dominated our cost of sales. Our contract was forged in the heart and written in blood. We were like brothers who trusted each other to the end, and we often fought like brothers, too! Still, we were bound by a common enemy, 3M. Shurtape competed with 3M in the industrial market, while Manco battled them at retail.

I'll never forget a time in the early 1980s when a mutual competitor of Manco and Shurtape's went bankrupt. In our separate markets, we were at the scene on the heels of the news, knocking on doors and picking up customers. But in perhaps the crowning moment of our partnership, Shurtape agreed to buy all of the defunct company's equipment with nothing more than a promise from Manco that we would work our tails off to bring home the volume. I'm forever indebted to that team and the way we fought side by side. I'll never forget the leaders of that company: Pope Shuford, Glenn Hilton, Dave Taylor, and Brad Dozier. Though Glenn and Dave have passed on, they are forever friends in my heart. To this day, the Shuford-Kahl family partnership lives on between my sons, John and Bill, and Pope's sons, Jim and Steve.

Some might say that this kind of relationship was for a different age, but I disagree. Twenty years does not define an age. Trust and values will always be the critical ingredients of any partnership, whether things are formally written on a piece of paper or not.

The leader must always be searching, probing, and hunting for ways to innovate and bring value to customers. Kim Clark, Dean of Harvard Business School, once said in an interview that a leader has "the ability to see value, often where others can't." Herb Kelleher of Southwest Airlines puts it this way: "The way I've always approached things is to be prepared for all possible scenarios of what might happen. I usually come up with four or five scenarios. I do this all the time. I do it in the shower. I do it when I'm out drinking."

No matter where you do your best thinking, go there often. Make sure you balance your demanding routine with the right dose of free time for your mind. My experience says that the best creative thinking, the purest expression of problem solving, happens *on the edge*. It happens in the borderland: between your business and your customer, your company and your supplier, your work and your family, your project and your vacation, your spreadsheet and your break in the cafeteria. Creativity is magnified where worlds collide. Like the plate tectonics that give birth to mountain ranges, colliding thoughts give rise to great ideas. The vacation doesn't make you more creative, but clearing your desk in preparation to leave, or the easy mind that returns with a fresh perspective on old problems, might.

Whatever we discover about the origin of life—the most creative event in our universe—we will surely discover that it happened on the edge, between swirling, colliding environments. So force yourself to engage the edges of your business. Your team will be doomed to struggle in the pit of mediocrity as a result of internalized, less-than-innovative thinking if you don't.

FORGING A STRATEGY

The truly great leader not only has a vision, but also defines a strategy to achieve it. Building a strategy is as much a product of the creative mind as creating a vision. But, as opposed to a vision, strategic thinking requires even greater knowledge of the world, and the *discipline* to turn that brainchild into a tangible plan.

As the path unfolds, obstacles and opportunities are encountered that were not clear at the start of the journey. Leader and team must react. Do they forsake the strategy? No! As George Patton said of battlefield encounters, "Strategy and tactics do not change; only the means of applying them are different." The leader must have the creative ability to think outside the box and adapt to developing situations. Capt. Michael McKean's definition of leadership echoes this wisdom when he says that a leader has "an ability to adapt to new behaviors very quickly." Many leaders have the knowledge but lack the creativity, the discipline, or the courage to make decisions that can make a difference when challenges are encountered.

I need to make a point about courage now, although I will touch upon it later. If creativity is to blossom, a leader needs courage. The leader needs to set aside his or her ego and risk failure. You can crush creativity under the weight of "analysis-paralysis"—or what I call *MBA-itis*. Delaying decisions as one searches for perfect information is a trap that captures the faint of heart and becomes an excuse for avoiding tough decisions. Make a decision and fix the mistakes as you go. Like General Patton said, "The best is the enemy of the good." The leader must be fortified by a certain amount of self-confidence and courage, ready to trust his or her ability to react to inevitable mistakes and changing conditions.

COMMUNICATING AND INSPIRING

Of course, it's not enough for a leader to simply have a vision, innovative ideas, and a strategy. He or she must communicate it to the entire team. A leader casts a vision, but that isn't to say that his ideas and goals are written in stone and carried down from the mountain. A leader may take the time to articulate the vision in writing, or he or she may simply let actions and decisions speak in their own, eloquent language. The good Lord knows that none of these options are better than the other. There are just as many "control freaks" who fail as leaders because they cling to their secret plans and visions as there are successful "quiet types" who inspire others, not with flowery words, but through bold actions. There are just as many charismatic, unethical flameouts as there are outspoken visionaries. Don't get hung up on personal style—not every leader needs to be the epitome of charisma. Get hung up being yourself and finding a way to achieve results.

In any case, a clearly articulated vision is the key to inspiring your team. Inspiration is about engaging the heart of the team and gaining their emotional commitment to the overall goal. To achieve such spirited energy in the face of myriad obstacles and challenges, people have to see a compelling vision of the future.

Don't just consider *how* you will articulate your vision, but make sure that the objectives are clear and consistent. It's tough to be consistent in the face of challenges, mistakes, setbacks, and the like. The leader must rise above the mayhem and ensure that the vision remains intact, no matter the strength of any storm. The leader may sometimes have to make short-term decisions that contradict the vision—leadership is often full of paradox—but even those decisions must be viewed as taking one step back to allow for two more steps forward. It's been said that the hallmark of genius is to hold two completely opposing thoughts at the same time and not lose your mind. I'm not sure if it's a sign of genius or insanity, but I do know that an effective leader needs to tread the line of paradox. Depending on how a situation unfolds, you need to be able to move in either direction.

Sticking to the vision when times are tough is probably more inspiring to the troops than a fiery speech. Courageous decisions and critical victories excite emotions and inflame passions. As humans, we are prone to embrace examples of heroism; seeing our leaders in action might be the closest we ever come to validating the dream of heroism we carry inside ourselves.

But not only is sticking to the vision inspiring, it also avoids the detrimental repercussions that ever-changing plans have on a team. A team needs consistency of vision and strategy—even when tactics shift—in order to sustain trust in their leader. Leaders who go flopping from idea to idea, instead of harnessing the inherent momentum that comes from focus, will lose credibility, burn their team's energy, and hinder their ability to maneuver effectively.

Holding true to your vision requires the conviction that your vision is right. Conviction is the basis for the courage it takes to stay the course. Michael Eisner, Disney's long-time CEO, has been quoted as saying, "Around here, a powerful point of view is worth at least 80 IQ points." Part of his point is that great ideas go nowhere without the courage and stamina to declare a position and stick to it. Let the team know your vision—your point of view—in clear and unambiguous terms, and have the courage to stay the course.

MOTIVATING THE TEAM

If inspiration is the stimulation of emotion, then motivation is turning those feelings into actions. Inspiration has to do with creating a vision of something bigger than the team. Motivation, on the other hand, has to do with little things. Motivation is about paying attention to the details and understanding what is important to people—things like saying thank you, recognizing a job well done, and celebrating achievement. Much has been said about not sweating the small stuff and focusing on big priorities, and there is much truth to the importance of that discipline, but another paradox of leadership is that the small stuff *really* matters to people. In fact, the "small stuff" is often "big stuff" in disguise.

Phil Jackson, former coach of the Chicago Bulls and the great Michael Jordan, said in a January 1996 *Industry Week* article, "Most leaders tend to view teamwork as a social-engineering problem: take X group, add Y motivational technique, and get Z result. In reality, the most effective way to forge a winning team is to call on the players' needs to connect with something larger than themselves." What Jackson is really saying is that sometimes inspiration is more important than motivation.

In the same article, Jackson described how the team reacted to the death of Scottie Pippen's father in the middle of a tough playoff series. In the locker room before a key game, the team gathered around Scottie and recited a prayer for him and his father. The team bonded during that special moment, and then they went out and won the game. The idea of winning the world championship may inspire, but actions, such as helping a struggling teammate, are what motivate.

Motivation often boils down to the simple fact that we all want to win and most of us want to have fun doing it. Break the rules sometimes. Encourage your mavericks. Reward the superstars. Get rid of the dead wood. Otherwise, you'll encourage a kind of cancerous, corporate socialism. Don't stifle your best folks by trying to keep the average people happy.

At Manco, we tried our share of stunts to have fun and keep our team motivated. I've swum across an icy pond in October, I've had my head shaved, and I've dressed up like a cowboy in a corporate video—all because I challenged my team to exceed their own expectations. Set your ego aside (did you get that message, yet?) and don't take yourself too seriously. Laughing at your successes and failures primes the emotional pump of everyone on the team. And the payoff? People just might enjoy their work and be less afraid to make mistakes. By bringing some perspective and excitement to the office, people might just forget those personal worries for a time being and answer the phone with a smile. Maybe they will even solve a tough problem for a customer without exploding with anger at their teammates from the pressure of pent-up frustration.

At Manco we managed individual motivation well. We compensated fairly, issued aggressive merit increases to our stars, and shared a lucrative bonus plan with everyone in the company. As Paul Brown said, "Motivation is like a fire. Unless you add fuel, it will go out." We added fuel to our partners' fires through a great recognition program that included attendance awards, service anniversaries, and "extra effort" awards that people won only by nomination from their bosses or colleagues. These were given out at a special meeting we held each month to review key financial results (sales, gross margin, net income) and champion our success as a team.

Individual rewards are necessary, but you can't stop there. When the team wins, find ways to celebrate your success *together*. One shining example came when Manco crossed the $100 million revenue threshold. We rented a theater in downtown Cleveland, hired Jeff Keller, who played the Phantom on Broadway longer than any other singer, and David Lai, who conducted *The Phantom of the Opera* for many years, and we put on the show of a lifetime. People who worked in our factory and had never seen Cleveland's Theater District put on their best clothes and joined our company's leadership for a night of Andrew Lloyd Weber's music. Some 2,500 people—more than four hundred of our own "partners," their families, and many great friends partied and reveled in the success we achieved together. There is no doubt about it—some of the motivation for working hard comes from playing hard.

One of Sam Walton's rules says something similar: "Think of new and more interesting ways to motivate and challenge your partners . . . Make bets with outrageous payoffs . . . Celebrate your successes . . . Find some humor in your failures . . . Loosen up, and everybody around you will loosen up."

One time, I sent Sam a book on motivation, and he wrote back to me with a personal version of the same message:

> *I want to thank you so much for the book . . . I know it will help us in so many ways in continuing to try to develop good morale, good attitude, and keep our folks motivated as we go down this tough old road of retailing. It has to be fun, as you well know, and that is what we all must keep uppermost in mind.*

A leader can only push so much motivation on people. A team that wants to be motivated has to be in place first. Recruiting the right people—people who have a burning desire to win—is probably the biggest prerequisite to being able to motivate others. One of the keys to Manco's success was that we never delegated recruiting to our Human Resources department (which we called *Partner* Resources). HR had a big role with administration and helping to systematize the recruiting process, but our battlefield leaders were the ones responsible for finding the talent they needed to get their jobs done. Recruiting is an executive responsibility.

At Manco, we built a heck of a "farm system" for meeting talented prospects. It happened almost by accident. As a graduate and Board member of John Carroll University, I developed a great friendship with the school's head football coach, Tony DeCarlo, Sr. Tony started sending kids my way—handpicking the best student athletes and sending them to Manco for interviews. We hired most of them. At one point, we had more than twenty-five JCU graduates working in our company, including Tony's son, Tony DeCarlo, Jr., one of the best salesmen we ever sent to the front line. Tony, Sr. had a hard time referring his son to me because he was a Sociology major with no business experience, but it turned out to be one of the best favors he ever did for me. Tony, Jr. built a strong business at several key retailers, including OfficeMax, a great Cleveland-area success story.

If you want to build a team that is not just responsive to motivation but that motivates itself, follow Herb Kelleher's advice about recruiting: "Seek people who have some balance in their lives, who are fun to hang out with, who like to laugh, and who have some non-job priorities, which they approach with the same passion that they do their work. Spare me the grim workaholic or the pompous, pretentious professional; I'll help them find jobs with my competitor."

Driven to Win

"The only sustainable competitive advantage is speed."

Jack Shewmaker, Director of Wal-Mart Stores and
Retired President

On a late spring day in 1973, I sat down in the quiet of my usually noisy living room and tuned in to the Belmont Stakes. My wife and five kids were out and about, and I took a break from my usual Saturday workload to watch Secretariat take a rare shot at winning the Triple Crown. What I saw left a permanent mark on my psyche.

It was one thing to recognize the moment that Big Red seemed to cement his claim to the title—somewhere on the backstretch, as he neared the top curve of the track—but it was quite another to see what happened next. With his competition no longer relevant, the horse turned his ambition loose. Chills washed through my body and the hair on my arms stood on end as I saw this wondrous animal push himself to be the best. What was astonishing, though, is that this intensity did not come from any external threat, but rather from some hidden, internal desire *to simply be the best.*

The sheer magnificence of those two minutes and twenty-four seconds overwhelmed me. The thrill and excitement of seeing such an exhibition of excellence kicked off an emotional chain-reaction that moved me greatly. I was deeply struck with humility, at once recognizing that my own habits and disciplines could never measure up to the greatness I had just witnessed.

In reality, it is easy to *say* that you embrace Socrates' wisdom that you "know nothing," but it is quite another to *feel* as humble as I did in those moments. As I stood to leave the room, my reeling mind centered itself on renewed commitments. I suddenly knew that the battles I fought were not against my competitors, but against myself. For the sake of my family and my team at Manco, I knew that I had to set new and higher expectations of myself as a leader. And I knew that the only way to achieve those expectations would be to invest in my responsibility as a student so that I could learn and relearn the lessons leading to greatness. I made a choice right then to always pursue my personal best. I made a choice to let my passion for success lead my decisions. I made a choice to lead with my heart.

A long time later, well after Secretariat had died, I heard that a necropsy discovered he had the biggest heart ever measured in a horse. It had nearly twice the capacity of a typical racehorse's heart, able to pump more blood through his oxygen-thirsty body than that of any other horse. What a fitting find! Secretariat simply had the heart to win.

I suppose many effective leaders find fuel for their desire to win through a focus on external competitors, but those who rely on external fuel walk a fine line. Preoccupation with outsiders can feed negative emotions and create bad habits. While anger, jealousy, fear, and other emotions can sometimes provide useful incentives, at high doses they can be dangerous to the health of a leader's organization. Such negative emotions can cause clouded, irrational judgments. They can impair character and cause egocentric decisions. They may foster a win-at-all-costs mentality, which can, ultimately, harm the integrity of the organization.

Truly great leaders compete against *themselves*. Their ambition springs from their desire to be the best—not necessarily the biggest, and not necessarily the most victorious, but the best. I'm not suggesting that a leader should ignore his or her competitors. In fact, a great leader must study and scrutinize the competition. However, when it comes to defining your team's capabilities and challenging the organization to succeed, you will do yourself a disservice if you build your vision around the other guy. President Kennedy's goal might have been to set a Cold War standard by making America the first country to visit the moon, but the nation's motivation to achieve that goal came from within. It came from the inner drive to achieve our collective potential. Beating the Soviets was just a by-product of realizing the greatness inside of us.

Sam Walton once said, "Commit to your business . . . I think I overcame my personal shortcomings by the sheer passion I brought to my work." Vince Lombardi, one of the greatest football coaches of all time, had much to say about passion and commitment. He claimed, "Battles are primarily won in the hearts of men." He also said, "Winning isn't everything. The desire to win is everything. In fact, it's the only thing." These great leaders knew that competitive passion is what separates the wheat from the chaff. Take yet another look at Capt. Michael McKean's definition of leadership. He says a leader has "a boundless energy to put learning into practice." Energy, drive, heart, passion—it is all the same thing. At Manco, we hung signs with the words of these men high on our walls so that we would never forget that the drive to succeed comes from the inside.

But drive is not just about thoughts and words; drive is transferred to a team through sheer *feeling*. A leader can't just say that he or she is passionate, and ask the team to come along; a leader must light the team's fire and compel them to engage their own ambition. I remember lighting the fire in one of Manco's young marketing partners just about the time our retail business began to accelerate. Back in the mid-eighties Bill Nicholson was running our Graphics Department—in fact, he *was* our Graphics Department! He worked from an old drafting board and a drawer full of art supplies. Bill came to me one day and told me he was struggling. He explained that he had dyslexia, and that his poor reading, writing, and spelling skills were causing him to question his talent and lose confidence in himself. As a former Eagle Scout, Bill wasn't satisfied with second best, so he reached out to me for help. He came to me not out of shame, but with the trust that I could help him succeed. I told him not to worry about bad spelling—that's why they invented spell-check. I told Bill to forget about his challenges, emphasize his strengths, and to only worry about developing his great skills.

He soon came back to me with a proposal to buy a new tool—an Apple Macintosh computer—so that he could bring a new kind of speed and quality to our design efforts. Bill saw the worth of a relatively new technology and how it could help him keep up with the hustle of our sales and marketing teams. He fought our CFO—there was no way to justify the investment financially—but with my support he got his wish. For weeks, he stayed at the office until midnight or later learning how to use that thing. Over the next ten years, Bill built a team of artists, with a slew of computers, into a crucial center of competence for our business. Bill eventually turned the reins of that department over to someone he had hired, someone he knew could do the job even better and take it further than he had. Then he went on to blaze trails for the company in the realms of photography and video production.

Our speed of packaging design, from concept to final art, was critical to the "time trial" product testing we conducted in retail stores. I remember one situation in particular when we got a phone call from a Wal-Mart buyer who gave us an idea. Ninety minutes later we e-mailed him concept images and were on the phone talking about the opportunity. We got a $1.5 million order because of that speed. And all of it began with that investment in Bill's talent. With that passionate investment in one man, Manco got an annuity of A+ effort in return.

When Sam Walton died in April 1992, I made the somber trek to Bentonville, Arkansas, to honor his family and memory. Early on the morning of his funeral, I filled a cup with coffee in the hotel lobby and turned to leave for the church. A man, whose big, strong body stood in contrast to the emptiness impressed upon his wrinkled face by grief, caught my eye. He was wearing a Wal-Mart badge.

I walked over to him and introduced myself and asked if he worked at Wal-Mart. He told me that he did not—as it turned out, he had never been to Wal-Mart. But he knew Mr. Sam well, for he had run Sam's hunting camp for more than twenty years. His name was Walter Sheil, and he quickly warmed to a conversation about his late friend.

Walter told me that he didn't know Sam as a businessman, just as a friend and hunter. Just as a man at play. I asked him about that, about how he would describe Sam's essence from knowing him on those intimate terms. He bit his lip and his great wrinkles deepened across his forehead. He thought for a minute, then said, "Sam asked for 110 percent all the time, and he gave you back 120 percent."

After our brief chat, I thanked Walter and asked him if I could use his comments in a eulogy I'd planned to write in Sam's memory. He said that was fine, and we wished each other well. As I neared my rental car in the parking lot, I heard Sheil's voice booming behind me.

"Mr. Kahl! Wait!"

I turned to see the big cowboy lumbering toward me.

"If you're gonna write this down, I want you to get it straight," he said. "Mr. Sam didn't ask for 110 percent. He *demanded* it. And then he still gave you back 120 percent."

It's one thing for a leader to be driven, but it's quite another to transfer that energy to the team and expect *everyone* to be the best they can be. People who knew and worked with Sam always say two things about the man: He was tough, but fair; and he drove them to achieve more than they thought they could.

People need to know—clearly and unequivocally—where you, as their leader, stand. Peter Drucker said that a leader is "a monomaniac on a mission." Don't be afraid to let the "maniac" out of the closet and get passionate about your business. Sure, you might ruffle some feathers if you get mad and scream and shout now and then, but you are just as likely to find that your best people will absorb your passion and energy and convert it into action and performance. Remember that the buck stops with you, and that few people will care about success as much as you do.

PASSION AND SPEED

True to Jack Shewmaker's words that open this chapter, I have no doubt that our competitive success at Manco was a direct result of our passion and speed. High speed was our default pace. At Manco, our culture revolved around eliminating wasted time, demolishing procrastination, and serving customers in real-time. When we got crushed with unexpected product demand, our salaried office team put on their jeans and packed boxes or loaded trucks. When our on-time service performance dipped for some reason, the entire company knew about it through our measurement and meeting systems—at Manco, we believed that bad news had to travel ten times faster than good news. Whenever we encountered a problem, swarms of people were there to find a solution, either with their brains or their brawn.

We extended this relentless, problem-solving attitude to our customers in many ways. I recall a time when a Wal-Mart store caught fire in Kentucky. We had a list of volunteers signed up and some were even en route from Cleveland to help reset the store before I could even issue the command. Dan Perella, our Vice President of Wal-Mart sales at the time, set aside his team's agenda and they spent nearly a week in that store: cleaning, erecting shelves, and stocking product. Through that experience, they bonded with the customer in immeasurable ways. Friendship, loyalty, teamwork, and goodwill permeated our relationship with Wal-Mart's home office and those grateful store associates. We had a great saying at Manco: "The speed of the leader sets the speed of the pack." In this case and many others, Dan set a pace that the rest of us at Manco had to keep up with.

The driven leader knows that speed is essential to success. There is often no substitute for being first to market with innovative ideas. As mentioned earlier, innovation fosters trust with your customers; they come to view you as someone who knows and anticipates their needs. If you're not leading the charge with innovation, your customers will not trust that you understand them, and unfortunately, your competitors will likely take the cake. Innovation earns trust. Sales and profits follow.

A great example of "Manco speed" happened when one of our Sales Account Managers, Dan Brogan, and our Marketing Director, Brian Vulpitta, were driving home from an important sales call. They had been trying to crack into a big account and finally got an order. Brian and Dan were a phenomenal team when they went to visit customers together. From their car, they called the Purchasing Manager back in the office, a young guy named Tom Donelan. They needed to alert him to the deal, so that Tom could fill the pipeline with product. Tom remembers Dan telling him that he had "good news and bad news." The good news was that they got the order; the bad news was that the customer wanted it to ship in four weeks. That was bad because the product was brand new, not in stock, and Brian had sourced the item from a supplier in Asia. Even worse news was that the customer wanted a special attachment, which the Asian supplier could not provide. It would have to be added at Manco.

Tom told Dan and Brian that he had some bad news of his own: it would be sixteen weeks before Manco even had the product in its warehouse. And that didn't count putting the attachment on the item once it got there. The three argued passionately about their options for a few minutes, then Dan ended the conversation by asking Tom to put the best possible plan together and they'd review it when he got to the office. Dan's final words on the phone were, "Remember, customers buy from us because we say *yes*."

Somehow, Tom and the rest of our operations team pulled that order together. Product literally came from all corners of the globe: some from Asia, some from distributors in America, some from Mexico. When our manufacturing team criticized Tom's action plan and complained about their task to put on the attachment, Tom threw his fist on a table and translated Dan's message about speed and why customers buy from Manco. The end result? The order shipped on time and complete.

Years later, Dan, Brian, and Tom all earned a place on our executive committee. Dan eventually became the company's Chief Operating Officer, succeeding my son, John, when he became CEO. Brian went on to lead the company's innovation as Vice President, New Product Development; and Tom became our Vice President, Operations, where he built that service mindset into his entire team and the systems they used.

Great leaders do not procrastinate—they solve problems in real-time, dealing with situations as they arise. I spent a day working with Tom Coughlin once and got a first-hand lesson in what I call *Leadership NOW*. Tom was in Cleveland for a local event when a crisis emerged at a Wal-Mart store they had just opened. We jumped into my car and rode over to the store. This store stood in the heart of a multi-ethnic community and served predominately African-American and Jewish customers. The problem with the store was obvious. Everything from the signage to the merchandise was geared toward white customers, who comprised only 22 percent of the store's market.

When we went inside, we spoke briefly with the manager. After less than four minutes, Tom excused himself to make a phone call. I could hear him telling Doug Degn, Wal-Mart's Executive VP of Merchandising at the time, to "Get up *to* Cleveland *today*!" (Tom used a few other colorful words, which I have chosen to omit!)

Tom took responsibility and action immediately, but he didn't blame anybody. He didn't look for a scapegoat to fire. He simply demanded that the problem be fixed fast. That day, five VPs flew from Bentonville to Cleveland and had an action plan framed for Tom before sundown. The manager, who had some skin in the game, was later reassigned. Of course, Tom's hurri-cane-like response to this particular problem was not meant solely to fix a single store, but to change the attitudes and overall system at Wal-Mart's home office, all of which affected count-less stores every day.

It was in that store that I first heard Tom use the term "store of the community." It is a phrase that became a mantra for Wal-Mart as it retooled itself to serve diverse shopping demographics. From problems at this one store in Cleveland, Tom was able to point an enormous company toward a focused direction of improvement. Through *Leadership NOW,* Tom was able to bring a sense of urgency to his company that no consultant or research report could ever match.

We left that store to visit a few others in the area. In the car, Tom continued to make phone calls to other Wal-Mart execu-tives regarding the situation. Between those calls, I handed Tom the resume of a bright, young buyer who I knew had worked for a west coast retailer. The young man had just taken a job with one of Wal-Mart's biggest retailing competitors in order to "take a step closer to Wal-Mart." After reading the resume and asking me a few questions, Tom pulled out his phone again and called the guy! Despite everything else going on that day, recruiting great people found its place in Tom's hectic schedule. In his words: "I don't want that kid spending one more day learning a bad culture if he wants to come to Wal-Mart."

Despite my bias toward speed, an obvious caution is due. There is no doubt that speed can kill, if it's reckless. The leader must understand the risks of speed. He must avoid acting hastily for the sole sake of being out in front. In the words of the great Chinese general, Sun Tzu, "While we have heard of blundering swiftness in war, we have not yet seen a clever operation that was prolonged." The leader must have the discipline to avoid reckless speed, but the drive to push his or her team forward . . . *and fast.*

TENACITY

Being a driven leader isn't just about going somewhere quickly, though. It's also about hanging in there when times get tough. It's about not giving up. The driven leader is committed to the mission and to the team that is pushing toward it—and he or she has to be tenacious in the face of adversity.

Our team sometimes felt overmatched by the deep pockets and sheer size of some of our competitors, especially 3M. Yet, from the executive meeting room to the key sales teams we put together, we drew strength from the idea that our persistence and tenacity could win battles. The words of Margaret Mead, the famous anthropologist, hung in our office to remind us that the odds weren't necessarily stacked against us: "Never doubt that a small group of committed people can change the world. In fact, it is the only thing that ever has." Sometimes we had to draw deep for the courage to keep going. The idea that we had a chance to make a real difference for our customers, to defeat the business-as-usual approach of our competitors, gave us the tenacity to stick it out when times got tough.

Courageous Leadership

"If the primary mission of a captain were to preserve his ship, he would never leave port."

Thomas Aquinas

There is no way to sugarcoat it: leadership can be frightening and lonely. As a leader, you will face threats and challenges that make your childhood monsters seem like petty daydreams. You'll experience problems that wake you with a cold sweat in the deep of night. These times are the defining moments, the crucibles that test your ability to make decisions and lead people. The aspiring leader will never reach his or her potential without the courage to step up and lead when it counts the most. When you find yourself in charge, you must confront your fears and show people the way despite them. As General Norman Schwartzkopf proclaimed in rule thirteen, "When given command, take command." Surely, taking command takes courage.

You might be wondering if you have the mettle to be a leader, if you have the courage to weather the inevitable storms you will encounter. Fear is a fundamental, motivating human emotion and we all experience it in different degrees. But courage is not measured against the degree to which we experience fear; courage is about remaining poised and acting effectively when you are afraid. General Patton said, "All men are frightened. The more intelligent they are, the more they are frightened. The courageous man is the man who forces himself, in spite of his fear, to carry on. Discipline, pride, self-respect, self-confidence, and the love of glory are attributes which will make a man courageous even when he is afraid."

Though tested most rigorously in the heat of battle, the leader's courage is not always revealed in a dramatic show of urgent decisions. Instead, it is practiced as one forges opinions and convictions about what is right for the team and then sticks to them. Courage is forged in the fires of those small, daily ethical questions, where you choose to define your principles; it comes from the heat of creative inspiration, where you craft a vision and chart a course. It takes real guts to win your own confidence and believe in yourself. The last of Sam's Ten Rules advises us to "Swim upstream. Go the other way. Ignore conventional wisdom . . . be prepared for a lot of folks to wave you down and tell you you're headed the wrong way. I guess in all my years what I heard more often than anything was: A town of less than 50,000 population cannot support a discount store for very long." It takes real courage to stick to your vision.

COURAGE AND CREATIVITY

I've heard it said that courage is the basis for creativity. I don't think it's the basis—I think an artistic, child-like mind is the basis for creativity—but courage is clearly a critical piece of the creative process. Quite simply, creative ideas go nowhere if a leader lacks the courage and stamina to withstand ridicule and assault. The simple act of taking that first, courageous step to share a novel idea or an experimental vision with others causes a chain reaction of events that can push and carry ideas further than they would travel without the wind of risk in their sails. Goethe said it well:

> *Until one is committed, there is hesitancy, the chance to draw back, always ineffectiveness. Concerning all acts of initiative and creation, there is one elementary truth the ignorance of which kills countless ideas and splendid plans: that the moment one definitely commits oneself, then providence moves too. All sorts of things occur to help one that would never otherwise have occurred. A whole stream of events issues from the decision, raising in one's favor all manner of unforeseen incidents, meetings, and material assistance which no man could have dreamed would have come his way. Whatever you can do or dream you can, begin it. Boldness has genius, power and magic in it. Begin it now.*

You can call it boldness or you can call it courage, but either way, creativity shrivels and dies without the actions that compel a team to strike down the path.

In 1982, Jack Shewmaker told me that raw guts proved to be the basis for many decisions at Wal-Mart. Sometimes a leap of faith is far more valuable than knowing the payback model or hurdle rate for a project. Financial gauges are important when it comes to establishing context and feasibility, but decisions always come from the gut.

The leader must exhibit plenty of courage just to set a vision and chart a course. Like Christopher Columbus, Magellan, or any great explorer, he or she must consider and accept the possibility of disaster. What's more, the leader must convince the team that the risk is worth it. As Sir John Harvey-

Jones said: "The task of leadership is to make the status quo more dangerous than launching into the unknown." The creative skills that the leader draws from to cast a vision and create a compelling case for change must be accompanied by the courage to go forth.

My oldest son, John, hung a sign above his office at Manco that reads, "Sounds dangerous . . . *Count me in!*" He wanted his team to know that he viewed danger and risk as opportunities. John knows that danger tends to lurk around the most exciting ideas, and subsequently, those ideas can lead to potential failure. But John also knows that taking those first uncertain steps will lead him to the borderland of the business, where the team is challenged and the learning process begins. John knows that taking chances and confronting danger is actually *less* risky than staying put or deferring the choice of action.

K. Erik Drexler, a leading technologist, has said, "Enlightened trial and error outperforms the planning of flawless intellects." Don't forget my term for intellectual constipation: *MBA-itis.* Don't slow down looking for perfection; you just won't find it. You need to give half-baked ideas a try. Bill Walsh, the great NFL football coach, put it this way: "The point isn't to be infallible, but to be right more than you're wrong."

There was a time at Manco when a young executive chose a name for an important new product. I absolutely hated his suggestion. It was tough for me to suck it up and tell him that I didn't agree with the name, but to go ahead and try it. I was scared to death; this particular product launch was one of our biggest and riskiest moves to date. In the end, though, I was more afraid of stifling the team by not allowing them to make their own choices, even at the risk of mistakes.

An effective leader needs to set aside his or her ego and go back to being a student who learns on the fly from the chaos generated by a team of trusted colleagues, ever ready to challenge the boundaries and put himself in harm's way.

COURAGE AND LEARNING

The Wal-Mart team offers a great example of how to set ego aside in order to learn from their mistakes. They have a process called "correction of errors," which they apply following key projects and their biggest seasonal cycles. The process involves a rigorous examination of measures of performance and key facts, and it requires a disciplined effort to attack areas of the system where breakdowns and mistakes occurred. Though sometimes awkward and uncomfortable for the participants, the folks at Wal-Mart know that the process is essential to the success of the entire team. Leaders and managers must set aside their titles and their personal interests to solve problems. In effect, they must learn what their business, their colleagues, and their customers are trying to teach them.

As I've said a few times in this book, setting aside your ego is crucial to learning. I truly believe that egotism takes root across an entire team when a leader lacks self-confidence. Self-confidence is a form of personal courage that allows a person to trust and believe in himself—not because the person knows himself to be perfect, but because he knows that he is able to find ways to compensate for his imperfections.

Personal courage is self-confidence, and self-confidence allows the leader to admit that he or she doesn't have all the answers. Furthermore, only a grounded ego will react well to failure. If you're caught up in your own self-importance, you'll be intolerant of your mistakes, and intolerant of the mistakes your team makes. When failure is punished because of such intolerance, the long-term result is obvious: everyone will tighten up and take less risk. Less risk taking means less creativity and innovation, which could ultimately cause the death of your organization. What's more, an egotistical leader will not take responsibility for mistakes, and thus, the great lessons which come from making mistakes will go unlearned.

Think about how you would help a child learn to ride a bike. You'd be patient and tolerant of mistakes. You'd encourage her to take risks, and console her when she falls. You'd instruct her about balance and turning the wheel, but you couldn't possibly teach her how to react when that sickening feeling of veering off course comes over her. If you think about it, a bicycle lesson is full of examples of courage: the child's courage, which springs from your encouragement, and the courage *you* exhibit when you introduce the potential for pain to someone you love. Notice also the crucial role of trust—the child's willingness to learn something new, her courage, and her self-confidence is inspired by her trust in you. She trusts how you'll react when bad things happen; she knows that you will not chastise her for falling off the bike, as you were the one who encouraged her to take the risk in the first place.

DEFINING MOMENTS

I've heard the following idea attributed to Warren Bennis, Ph.D., the well-published teacher of business leadership from the University of Southern California: Leaders learn how to lead by being stuck in a tough situation and fighting their way out. They encounter at least one *crucible* event that forges their mettle as leaders. Of course, for every leader who emerges stronger from such a trial, there are perhaps hundreds, maybe thousands, of people who succumb to the intense pressure and fail.

I look back at my career and see several such defining moments. As a child I learned many lessons the hard way. In business, I went through my first crucible when the owner of the company I worked for cheated me out of the money I was due on my commission check for the fourth or fifth time. With small kids running through the halls of a new home we'd owned for a week, I took a stand. I decided that integrity was something I was not willing to negotiate. Rather than justify a cheated paycheck and rationalize my boss's faulty values, I called him and quit. I was terrified, and my wife was scared and angry. After three frightening days of uncertainty, my boss called me back with an offer to sell me the company. I put down my last $10,000, took out a loan for another $182,000, and became the owner and CEO of the company. I shortened the name of the business by taking the initials of the former owner, renaming the company Manco.

It takes real courage to make a decision that scares you to death, but you have to do it if you want to be an authentic, trustworthy person. You must have rock-solid integrity and sound values. Believe me, your team will never examine your decisions as closely as when times are tough and there is a gun to your head. They want to know how you perform under pressure because they know that the business of leadership is full of it. They want to know if you can make the tough choices, or if you try to find the "easy way out," bending the rules when it suits you. And it's not just about moral values. Nothing inspires a team more than courageous decisions, perhaps because we are all so psychologically attracted to acts of heroism. Surely Winston Churchill's decision to stay in London with his people during the incessant German bombing of the city inspired their very survival. That great leader faced the same risks as his countrymen. He walked the streets after those terrifying raids to encourage, console, and inspire them.

The first sign I ever hung at Manco read, "Successful people invest in themselves." More than anything else, I think my defining moments taught me to trust myself. While that philosophy is the essence of entrepreneurship, it also demonstrates the kind of courage it takes to be a leader of any sort.

ON BECOMING AN ENTREPRENEUR

Perhaps the ultimate test of courage is found in the experience of stepping away from the structured, stable conditions of career employment and into the uncertain world of entrepreneurship. A cold sweat drenched my body after I closed the deal to buy Manco. I tossed and turned night after night, kept awake by a fear that I had never felt previously. I worried I would let my family down, I worried that I was being irresponsible, and as a young father duty-bound to the well-being of his children, I was terrified.

I've heard people say that most entrepreneurs don't view themselves as risk takers; that they believe in themselves and their opportunity so completely that they don't truly appreciate the gambles they take. I could probably write an entire book on the experience of entrepreneurship itself, as it is a distinct subset of leadership that cannot be given its due in a few short paragraphs, but I must say this: While it is true that entrepreneurs probably don't identify many of the specific risks that others might see, that doesn't mean they don't see themselves as risk takers. When I made my choice, I knew it was a huge risk. I didn't make a list of everything that could go wrong, but I understood the high stakes at play. I fully grasped the consequences of failure. It meant losing everything and putting my family in jeopardy.

My father was surely an inspiration for my plunge into the unknown. I saw my dad build a dual career with a salaried job at American Greetings Corporation, the creative greeting card company based in Cleveland, and a job selling real estate on weekends. We never saw him on Sundays during open house hours. He worked hard to elevate our economic position, and as I've said, it was from him that I learned the value of a sound work ethic. I often heard my mother ask him why he couldn't stay home a few Sundays, and he always gave her the same answer: "Margaret, when you work on commission, you get zip for zip. I have to be there when lightening strikes. I have to make myself available to the opportunities."

Years of watching my dad work his butt off to help our family live comfortably imbedded a philosophy of hard work right into my soul. But aside from the value of a good work ethic, I learned something just as important: the value of entre-preneurship. Over the years, my father built his sales business to the point where he was earning more in commissions than he was at his job at American Greetings. One day he made the choice to quit that safe, comfortable job for the promise of earning more fruit for his labor. He went into real estate full time. I am forever indebted to my old man for teaching me about real courage and the importance of trusting in yourself.

LEADING CHANGE

If displays of battlefield courage provide natural sparks of inspi-ration, the opposite might be true of the effort to convince a team to move from comfort to peril. Organizations and their teams generally view their goals as achieving some kind of status quo—probably because the notion of "settling down" is so prized by our culture.

Of course, settling down can also be an indication of other things, too. In *The Road Less Traveled,* M. Scott Peck suggests that laziness might actually be original sin. We naturally tend to resist change and cling to the status quo, probably for a number of reasons: a deeply rooted survival instinct, an inherent laziness, fear of the unknown, or simple comfort with the way things are.

That said, a leader is someone who constantly makes the case for change and works against the natural human inertia of wanting to set up camp and stay awhile. The truly great leader knows that success springs from a nomadic lifestyle; his vision is of a winding path filled with discovery, learning, and opportunity. It's all about the journey. There really is no destination.

I've heard a great many leaders speak about change and creating an imperative for change in the hearts of their teams. In the 2000 General Electric annual report, Jack Welch wrote, "We've long believed that when the rate of change inside an institution becomes slower than the rate of change outside, the end is in sight. The only question is when."

When change is needed—and it almost always is—the effective leader must convince the team that they're standing on a "burning oil platform" and that they will fail if they do not alter their course. The burning platform metaphor comes from a real-life example of an oil platform that exploded in the North Sea in the late 1960s. Out of hundreds aboard, only two men survived. One of those who lived had jumped from the high platform into the frigid waters below—an action that the crew was repeatedly counseled against during their training, no matter the emergency they might face. If the fall didn't kill them, they were told hypothermia would. When this survivor was asked what compelled him to jump despite knowledge of his likely fate, he replied, "I chose probable death over certain death."

The leader needs to communicate a vision that compels the team to realize a future that they would otherwise not achieve. The leader's charge is to inspire feelings of greatness and tap into that burning desire to win inside all of us. He or she must convince the troops that they are faced with a mandate to change, progress, succeed, and survive.

COURAGE AND THE BURDEN OF LEADERSHIP

It takes great courage for a leader to face the fear of loneliness. The old cliché is right: it *is* lonely at the top. Margaret Thatcher, the former leader of the United Kingdom, said, "Being Prime Minister is a lonely job . . . You cannot lead from the crowd." Your job is not to win a popularity contest, but to earn trust and respect as a leader. That means making tough decisions—decisions that may win or lose a popular vote, and in any case, will probably never please everyone simultaneously. There are some lonesome moments before, during, and after decisions are made, when the leader confronts the burden of great responsibility.

It has also been said that leaders, like eagles, don't flock. They may know many people, but the best leaders have few close friends. Of course, I am hard pressed to say whether or not this is so, but it makes sense to me for two reasons. The first is that building true friendships requires time and attention, of which the driven leader has precious little. The second reason is that close friendships can bring great complexity to the process of making tough decisions, and the leader knows that he or she must maintain an objective viewpoint in order to steer the organization toward success. Intimate friendships can become an obstacle to the sound, objective decision making leadership demands.

COURAGE IS CAUTIOUS

Do not confuse courage with recklessness. Sometimes, the most courageous decision is to abandon an opportunity or to turn away from a risk that is too great. Tzu-lu, the master Chinese military general and contemporary of Sun Tzu, said, "The man who was ready to beard a tiger or rush a river without caring whether he lived or died—that sort of man I should not take. I should certainly take someone who approached difficulties with due caution. . . ."

Millennia later, General Patton said basically the same thing: "There is a time to take counsel of fear, and there is a time to forget your fears . . . When you have collected all of the facts and fears, make your decision. After you make your decision, forget all of your fears and go full steam ahead."

Though the stakes may be high, there are remarkable victories awaiting the patient leader who surveys the landscape and takes timely action in full awareness of the pros and cons of his decisions. To triumph over fear is glorious in itself, for no other triumph could be achieved without this initial battle.

A Caring Culture

"No man stands taller than when he stoops to help a child."

Unknown

I'll never forget the time my youngest son, Bill, met Sam Walton. Bill had just graduated from John Carroll University—the same Jesuit university in Cleveland I attended—and had planned to take some time off before coming to work at Manco. He was looking forward to some relaxing vacation travel, but I had other plans for him.

I'd decided that Bill would take over my responsibility as Manco's lead salesperson at Wal-Mart. The day after his graduation ceremony, I was due to attend a Wal-Mart sales meeting down in Florida. I knew that Sam and other Wal-Mart executives would be there, and that it would be a great opportunity for Bill to meet some of the top brass. So we changed Bill's travel schedule and flew down to Florida together.

Sure enough, we met Mr. Sam. Sam could have just exchanged a pleasant greeting and moved on—Bill would have been happy just to shake his hand—but Sam put his arm around Bill and the two of them walked down the aisle alone for a few minutes. Sam asked Bill about school and about his hopes for his new job; they talked a bit about Wal-Mart and retailing. A few weeks later, Sam wrote to me, again taking the time to care about the personal details:

It was so good seeing you in Miami. I especially enjoyed meeting your fine son. I know you are very proud of him and his accomplishments, as well. You folks continue to do an excellent job as one of our primary suppliers. We compliment you for it.

In a single, aisle-way conversation, Sam ignited Bill's desire to win for Wal-Mart, and it was such a simple fire to light! All Sam had to do was show Bill that he *cared* about him; that Bill was worth a few minutes of Sam's time. Sam cared enough to ask a few questions and to offer a bit of advice. From that day on, whenever Bill was challenged to adapt Manco to Wal-Mart's needs and faced internal politics and inertia to make it happen, he put aside his competitive nature and made it personal: he wanted to serve Sam because Sam cared.

Seven months after Bill's first meeting with Sam, Bill and I and another Manco executive traveled to Wal-Mart for some meetings. We were leaving our hotel just after 6:00 a.m. when we spotted Sam in the lobby. He greeted all of us by name, including Bill, whom he'd met only once and had not seen in seven months. It's simply amazing how much of success springs from the human bond of friendship and respect, and how much those relationships depend upon simple things, like remembering someone's name. Nothing screams "you are important to me" louder than paying attention to these kinds of personal details.

Listening could be the key to making others feel important, and Sam Walton turned listening into an art. He often pulled out a pad of paper or a tape recorder and converted an idea from a floating thought to a concrete opportunity. Imagine the domino effect of this simple habit. Sam motivated countless associates by validating the worth of their ideas. He constantly reinforced the impression that Wal-Mart is a company that listened to its staff; and as a result, associates were more likely to be open and receptive to accept new goals, directives, and policies of the organization in the future. No other act tells an employee that you care about them and that you are their *servant* more than authentically listening to what they have to say.

In one of our early company videos, my son John said, "People do business with people." As Manco's Vice President of Sales, John knew all about what it took to earn trust and win business. Even as a Vice President, he personally handled Ace Hardware, one of Manco's longtime top accounts. John never wanted to get too far from the people behind the business. For John, and many other leaders at Manco, doing business was not about maintaining a relationship between a supplier and a customer—two artificial, legal entities—but about nurturing a relationship between a salesperson and a buyer. In fact, a leader must attend to and care for the myriad relationships business entails, from the front office, to the sales, marketing, technology, operations, and accounting department.

How many executives get tied up with the numbers and their busy schedules and forget that leadership is about people? Jack Shewmaker, one of the most intelligent and intense leaders I have ever met, has said, "I don't care how much you know until you show me how much you care." This perspective is a two-way street. As a leader, Jack wants to know about your heart, your desire to succeed by caring about the team—and you can bet your bottom dollar that the folks looking to be led want to know how much you care about them. They want to see your face. They want you to ask about their family. They want you to remember their names.

CULTURE, CULTURE, CULTURE
(OR, *SWEAT THE SMALL THINGS!*)

The little things are sometimes the most important things, for they hold the key to motivating a team to accomplish the big things. Like a clump of snow that drops from the branch of a mountain tree and grows into a full scale avalanche, the little things accumulate and give the organization mass and momentum in one direction or another. The little things become your *company's culture*. But what is culture?

Culture is a set of attitudes, beliefs, and values that spring almost solely from the aggregate of every little thing a leader says or does. Some people mistakenly believe culture to be unimportant—it is "soft" and nearly impossible to quantify—but I disagree. It's one of the most important things for a leader to understand, especially for the leader of a large or growing team. Culture also defines the organization's readiness for action and capacity for speed. By maintaining a hyper-vigilant focus on the little things, the leader ensures that the team is ready to handle the big things when they inevitably explode onto the scene. In this way, culture is a sort of never-ending boot camp that keeps the team's intensity high so that they are ready to swiftly execute whatever steps need to be taken when that red-alert button is pressed.

Let me give you an example of what I mean by this. Earlier, I mentioned that Manco sent some of our folks down to Kentucky to help a Wal-Mart store that had caught fire. The decision was made because everyone knew that the Manco *culture* revolved around that sort of speed and caring. There were plenty of other examples, too. For example, whenever a hurricane threatened to strike somewhere in the United States, our team went on high alert. Not because we were threatened by the weather in Cleveland, but because some-where on the continent, our customers' stores were. We stood ready with inventory and logistics, shipping Duck® Tape to the stores in the path of the storm so that people in those regions had the product they needed to protect their homes. Our everyday discipline of speed and service translated into moments of peak performance when our little company helped others in the face of natural disaster.

Interestingly, weather always played a key role in our busi-ness, and not just when Duck® Tape was needed to seal windows in a storm. We sold seasonal home insulation products, which depended on cold weather for sales. Because of this, we were always balancing on a precarious tightrope of inventory. Mother Nature could wreak havoc on our financial statements if we had too much or too little stock available. Our Wal-Mart sales team, led by Dan Perella, turned to the Internet and the National Weather Service to model weather patterns and ready themselves to deploy inventory to the right stores. On a daily basis, they worked closely with Wal-Mart's buying staff to "co-manage" inventory replenishment, often ignoring the Wal-Mart system's recommendations, which *reacted* to actual sales, in favor of pushing inventory to the stores by *predicting* the demand weather patterns would create.

At one point, a young analyst who worked under Dan's direction designed a computer model that linked up to every weather monitoring station in the country and applied some pretty slick math based on latitudes and longitudes to model store-specific weather patterns. Wal-Mart's own information technology team told the young man that his idea would require several hundred thousand dollars to program. A few weeks later, after some long nights and a lot of personal time, that young analyst delivered a homemade desktop application that was better and cheaper than even Wal-Mart could construct. *Caring becomes passion; passion becomes speed.*

Culture is a product of leadership. Only the top leader of an organization can establish its culture. Though the entire leadership team can influence the culture, enhancing it or undermining it, they still operate within the framework set by the top dog. In fact, they are in their positions only because of the top dog! The top dog sets the cultural tone through the many elements of leadership: student leadership, creativity, trust, drive, courage, caring, and discipline. Each of these things has something to do with culture.

Let's take a look at some questions to underscore the pervasive sources of culture. You'll know what the answers should be:

- Do the leader and the organization encourage learning and professional development with the right job requirements, training budget, and associate benefits?
- Do the leader and the leadership team communicate plans, budgets, and results within the context of ultimate, big picture goals on a regular basis?
- Does the company ship product before quality assurance testing is complete or regulatory approval officially earned?
- Are people rewarded for outstanding performance? Are they held accountable for a breech of corporate values and expectations?
- Do people feel comfortable taking risks and suggesting improvements to the operation, or are they sullen, stifled, and going through the motions?

- Are the bathrooms clean? Is the facility well kept and tidy? Is there a double standard of amenities, or do all associates work in equally tasteful conditions?

Culture is not found in a grandiose vision statement. It is established by habit and routine. Culture is the result of every decision, every day. These habits and routines become the cement binding people as a team. A culture creates momentum around ideas, values, mores, and becomes a governing force in its own right—and the right culture can lead to financial success for the organization overall.

I want to give you a simple example of how culture affected our bottom line at Manco. Early in our history we instituted a travel policy that required two travelers to share a hotel room (given that they were the same gender, of course!). Our policy—which we adopted from Wal-Mart—was designed to imbed a philosophy of cost control within the psyches of our troops. The policy was not merely meant to control travel costs, it was meant to deliver a message that we expected our company to get the most from any penny spent.

Cultural habits like this bring people together so that the vision of the leader becomes a vision shared by the entire team. The power of a team is geometrically greater than that of a group of fragmented individuals. As Franklin D. Roosevelt said, "People acting together as a group can accomplish things that no individual acting alone can ever hope to bring about." I felt so strongly about the importance of teamwork that I created an award around the idea, and it became Manco's highest honor. In a fit of inspiration one day, I scrawled the words that would become the basis for our Spirit Award: "To climb small hills and mountains can be done alone. To climb the highest mountain takes a team based on faith, trust, and honesty. Together let us climb the highest mountain." The Spirit Award is bestowed annually to select recipients who accomplish great things, not on their own, but through leadership and teamwork.

At Manco, an important aspect of our culture was engaging every single person and every single idea with full appreciation and respect. We made sure to get the countless, little things right in order to encourage the philosophy of "people first." I made sure I walked the halls of the office and the aisles of our production and distribution areas so that people knew I was accessible. On top of just being visible to our troops, I listened and reacted to their suggestions and concerns. On occasion, I felt that it was my job to bring a machete to the overgrowth of systems and people and management structures. Sometimes I knew instinctively where to cut, but mostly, the team pointed me toward problems. It is not enough to *say* that you have an open door; you need to throw it open and roll out the red carpet for each and every person. Only then will you be exposed to the real problems inside your organization. With all of the demands on my time and all of the topics competing for my attention, I admit that I never made the rounds as frequently as I should have. However, our Thursday meetings were helpful complements to facilitate the culture of our company; we expected our entire team to share information back and forth whether I was involved or not.

There are other ways, though, to assure that you hear what your team has to say. Don't overlook your most trusted ministers of culture. You know who they are: those people on your team who are unusually adept at taking the pulse of the organization and bringing you information about the troop's spirit when you haven't had the time or the inclination to go get it yourself. In our company, my daughter, Annie, was our divining rod of culture. She could smell a rat or recognize a go-getter quicker than any other leader on our team—and maybe because she was my daughter, she was quick to come to me with "recommendations" for change. Annie always brought a spirited conversation into my office. She even had the courage to confront the problems that originated with me. She was not afraid to tell me what to fix and when to fix it. She wasn't the only leader on her team that could stand up to a passionate, stubborn entrepreneur like me (and we all need those people who can set us straight once in a while); but she was the one who was most in tune with Manco's culture. That was probably because our company's culture was a projection of our family's culture, which Annie learned at home.

Another great technique we discovered for gaining the full attention and participation of our team was to use the four walls of our building. That's right: *the walls*. We turned our building into a locker room of sorts, literally bringing the walls to life. As you've realized by now, we hung famous quotations and motivational signs on nearly every square inch of open space, and the walls communicated our culture and our expectations to out partners all day long. Our associates always appreciated the motivation. Through the years, countless people have told me that those signs made them *think*; often helping them crystallize their ideas. Some have even told me that, on a bad day, seeing the right dose of motivation when they turned a corner picked them up a little.

One element of culture that has always intrigued me has to do with informal systems of communication. I have already mentioned the importance of clear communication surrounding an organization's strategy, goals, and objectives, but I wouldn't want anyone to think that "communication" is only about speeches, memos, or signs on the walls. Oftentimes, it has much more to do with hallway dialogue, airplane conversations, and even barroom banter.

The reality is that most corporate communication is informal, and it is in these settings that people are tuned in and receptive to ideas. Personally, I've always been amazed to witness the power of *stories*—anecdotes and tales of the past that humanize the team's leadership, and somehow connect the organization's vision for the future with the practical realm of real people, real situations, and what really happened in the past. I was continually astonished by how the stories of Manco's dramatic past made their rounds through the company. As new people joined our team, traveled together on business trips, and had fun socializing with their colleagues at lunch or after work, they were bombarded with an oral history of the company.

One particular story, which I always enjoyed hearing, happened while I was away. During a company-wide meeting, my son, John, and another fellow, who was our CFO at the time, got into a heated exchange in front of the entire organization. Their argument spilled into an animated post-meeting "discussion," which could be heard up and down the hallway. While these kinds of discussions between executives were rare, they weren't exactly groundbreaking. What made this particular argument unique was that the issue triggering it had something to do with the CFOs distrust of our people—he wanted to install a new policy that tightened the rules in such a way that our people would surely have felt as though they weren't trusted with basic matters.

John, on the other hand, voted in favor of our people. Instead of quiet resistance, he showed the people that he was on their side by choosing to disagree with the CFO in front of everybody—after all, the CFO had made the choice to raise the topic in front of everybody. What's so intriguing is that nearly everyone has a different version of the events: John said this, the other guy said that, then John did this, and the other guy did that. No matter the spin on the story, the same points always come across: Manco puts its people first, even sometimes at the expense of productivity; and that was the day that John Kahl, once a sales executive and the son of the CEO, became a leader and cultural force in the company.

Oral traditions are just one contributing element of culture. Culture has to do with your habits, and like leadership itself, it is holistic. It emerges from a complex set of characteristics and conditions. Culture could be the single most powerful force at work in an organization: it is nothing less than the ecosystem of human relationships within the business. If people and their performances are the only things that set companies apart, then establishing the right culture is a significant step toward success. Unfortunately, in our hard-wired world, who has time for something as intangible as how people "feel" about their work environment?

I'll tell you who has the time: the great leaders do.

CARE MOTIVATES

Sam Walton and Wal-Mart provide so many examples of how caring for people translates into a successful company. Two of Sam's Ten Rules have everything to do with caring. He writes, "Nothing else can quite substitute for a few well-chosen, well-timed, sincere words of praise." Sam knew what we all know: personal communication motivates people. He took it a step beyond what most of us do. By recognizing that caring is a factor in an organization's success, Sam developed a zealous discipline and forged the right habits around a notion most of us take for granted.

Another of Sam's Ten Rules says, "Share your profits with all your associates, and treat them as partners. In turn, they will treat you as a partner." In other words, you have to put your money where your mouth is. Share the wealth—at least with the key performers who deserve the rewards.

Throughout my career at Manco, I put a great deal of emphasis on treating people as partners. In the mid-eighties, I sold a chunk of stock to an Employee Stock Ownership Plan (ESOP) and began distributing wealth to our employees, who were called "partners" from that day on. Many "experts" felt that I was being too generous, perhaps downright foolish by establishing the plan, and they were quick to tell me so. On a wintry Cleveland day in 1991, however, when Sam Walton visited our company, I felt vindicated. During a tour of the facility, Sam turned to me and said, "Jack, I know what makes Manco a great company. The heart and soul of Manco are your people."

Sometimes the old clichés are right; the more you give, the more you receive. The greatest day of my life was when I sold the company and we wrote checks for all of those people who had helped us succeed. From the $192,000 I paid for the business in 1971, Manco grew into a global company valued at $90 million—$27 million of which belonged to our partners through that ESOP. They had helped to create the wealth and they deserved their share of the riches.

THE BIGGEST PICTURE

Caring is what ties leadership to the human condition. Showing that you care about others through your actions is an exercise so important that in *The Road Less Traveled*, perhaps the best-selling popular psychology book of all time, M. Scott Peck suggested the effort is nothing less than the definition of love itself. He said that love is an "active effort" to help another person grow and achieve their potential. Some might argue that Peck was writing about helping people grow *spiritually*, not career-wise, but I'd challenge them to show me the line between our spiritual lives and everything else we do while we're awake. Our jobs, our hobbies, our friends, our families—everything we do defines our spiritual lives, and whatever anybody does to help another succeed is an act of love.

Lest you think this sounds too soft, let me assure you that I am a devout capitalist who believes in the power of economic evolution and the "survival of the fittest business model." I believe in competition and the creative power of conflict. That said, I also firmly believe that a powerful byproduct of focused, responsible business management is that people find their own successes. Helping others to succeed—perhaps by creating jobs that enable people to provide for their families, or maybe by helping people to learn new skills, or to embrace the full potential of their capability—just might be what life is all about. The leader profits from his or her efforts to care in more ways than one. Not only is the organization enhanced, but the lives of the people who makeup that organization are also enhanced. Think about the domino effect of sending people from a workplace that reinforces these important values back to their homes and their communities. The "pay it forward" effect extends the stamp of the leader to countless people. Anita Roddick, founder of The Body Shop, said, "I want to work for a company that contributes to and is part of the community. I want something not just to invest in. I want something to believe in." The best leaders know that work is just a part of life. Building a corporate culture that engages the hearts of everyone on the team could be the most crucial secret of success.

When I asked Sam Walton if he would share what he felt was his greatest accomplishment with me, he put it this way: "I guess it would be helping to raise the esteem of so many folks." It is true that Sam demanded 110 percent, as Walter Sheil said, but it was Mr. Sam's attention to the motivating details of a caring corporate culture—all those little things that add up to so much that caused people to meet his expectations. His choice to care about others relentlessly—to lead with his heart—is what moved ordinary people to unleash potential they didn't even know they had.

Execution is the Thing

"I skate to where the puck is going, not to where it's been."

Wayne Gretzky, *The Great One*

A leader can have all of the traits of leadership illustrated so far, yet still fail to lead effectively. The servant leader needs one last, crucial trait to bind together all the others, and that trait is personal discipline. With personal discipline, a leader converts his potential into reality. With discipline, a leader takes plans and ideas and *executes* them. Discipline is the Duck® Tape that bonds a leader's traits into a single, unified expression of personality and style. It does not matter what a leader's respective strengths and weaknesses are in regards to specific elements of leadership, but it does matter that a leader knows those strengths and weaknesses well, and continually calls upon self-discipline to summon strengths and cover weaknesses.

Discipline is self-control. It is a self-imposed adherence to a set of behaviors, habits, or actions that are deemed important. Discipline provides the focus and self-restraint that leads to integrity and self-respect, and thus, makes it possible for a leader to emerge. How many excellent students do you know who can't commit the time and rigor to their study? How many creative people have you seen stray from idea to idea, unable to stick with one long enough to see it bear fruit? How many people *say* that they care about people, but never bother to follow their words and intentions with the right actions? Discipline is the tool of force that we use upon ourselves to delay gratification and confront the hard work that leads to results. Actually, discipline is not just a single tool, but a set of tools.

DISCIPLINE NO. 1: KEEP THE CUSTOMER FIRST

Perhaps the most important discipline is staying close to your customers and understanding their needs. Too often, organizations get caught up in their own internal complexity and forget that customers are the only reason they turn the lights on every day. The leader must enforce the discipline to maintain a high level of customer awareness in all areas of the company. Corporate arrogance must be banished from the sales and marketing teams, otherwise they will be unable or unwilling to listen to the customers' real needs and wants. Other teams must develop goals and indicators that are service based, and those teams should be rewarded according to performance. Contact with customers must be encouraged across all levels and functions.

A leader must relentlessly define and redefine how his or her company delivers value to the customer. Whether the value is cost efficiency or high fashion, it must be reinforced by everything your team does. Your people, their habits, your facilities—it all has to reinforce the value you want to communicate to your customers. Defining value becomes a habit like any other, and your focus will keep your team close to your customers' expectations.

The task, then, is to challenge your team to exceed your customers' expectations. Once you create the discipline to stay close to your customers, their needs, and how they view your firm, you must still go farther to give them the creative innovation they expect. Exceeding customers' expectations is one of Sam's Ten Rules. Customers expect and appreciate consistency, but they are loyal to the great feelings that spring from surprise and unexpected success.

THE DISCIPLINE OF PLANNING

The leader must have the discipline it takes to study the world and to learn. He or she must be able to turn good ideas into a vision, a vision into strategy, and strategy into plans and tactics. That's right: plans and tactics. And budgets. Planning is like going to the dentist. Everybody hates it, but it must be done, and it takes discipline to get it done. Many people ask what good is a plan when it's bound to change? To paraphrase Dwight D. Eisenhower, a plan might be worthless, but the process of planning is essential. The *discipline* of thinking about how a vision can become a reality sharpens that vision and makes it practical. Planning forces you to answer the question: What do we do next? The leader must cultivate the habits that lead to success. Planning is a habit. Monitoring progress on plans is a habit. Watching internal and external environmental indicators is a habit. Caring for the team is a habit. Like it or not, your habits and behaviors define you. Your actions, not your thoughts, are what people see. Furthermore, they define how much you learn, how much you inspire and motivate, and how much you care. Through disciplined habits and routines, the leader builds a team that understands its goals, knows its strengths, and accepts its limits. The discipline of planning also positions the organization to make the most worthwhile investment decisions. Making balanced investments that serve the many different areas of an organization is a difficult task. It's a manifestation of the most fundamental law of economics: allocating scarce resources to unlimited wants and demands. Understanding options, prioritizing, and making choices can be correlated to numerous elements of leadership, such as learning, creativity, courage, and so on, but it takes real discipline to ultimately ensure that the organization picks the most judicious path.

Jack Shewmaker has said to me (and many others) time and again that one of the most crucial keys to an organization's success is its ability to understand available technology and apply prudent solutions to advance the business and enhance its core competency. He knows that information technology is no panacea. A "system" must be built around great people and effective processes; technology comes later, and is often applied only as an enabler.

For instance, in the early 1980s, Jack made the choice to push Wal-Mart into outer space with the company's first investment in satellite communications. He fought hard to make the investment happen, even against the fears of Mr. Sam himself. Jack and his executive team viewed speed of communications as a core, competitive advantage at Wal-Mart. Jack simply felt that satellite technology could enhance a culture of fast-moving information and knowledge. He wasn't investing in technology for its own sake or trying to force new techniques into the company; he was trying to find a faster, more efficient way of connecting the stores to the home office. In fact, what he was doing was trying to find new ways to meet old goals. Given the costs, risks, and often painful change of technology implementation, Jack could not have stayed the course without great management discipline.

THE DISCIPLINE OF MANAGEMENT

Abraham Lincoln said, "If I had six hours to chop down a tree, I'd spend four of them sharpening my axe." A leader must ensure that the team's axe is always sharp. Performance must be objectively measured, clear expectations need to be set for each person, and clear, consistent feedback has to be delivered. Team members need to know what to expect, and they depend upon consistent messages from the top. Clarity of expectations builds trust. Visions are great, but marching orders are what the team needs in order to act *now*. In other words, a leader must be absolutely confident that the organization is *managed*. As Peter Drucker said, "The only things that evolve by themselves in an organization are disorder, friction, and malperformance."

Ironically, leaders rarely make the best managers. But they won't be the best leaders either, unless they learn to respect the need for managerial discipline and surround themselves with people who *can* manage. Andrew Carnegie said, "It marks a big step in a man's development when he comes to realize that other men can be called in to help him do a better job than he can do alone." To paraphrase similar wisdom from Malcolm Forbes: The job of the Chief Executive is to have people who are better than he is at every single aspect of the corporation's work. Notice how building the right team connects back to setting aside your ego and being a student; slice it whichever way you like, it all comes down to knowing yourself and your limitations.

No matter the type of organization you are leading, and regardless of the product or service it delivers, at its heart, your organization is nothing more than a collection of people working as a team. A leader must be second to none when it comes to managing the system that recruits and retains people for the organization. In a sense, a leader must replicate himself or herself across all boundaries and levels of the team—even into areas that are far removed from his or her areas of core competence. After launching a venture of any sort, a leader's number one job might be to invest in continuity. Succession planning is important to any team. It starts, not as a plan, but as a commitment to hiring and developing the right team to begin with. With the team in place, formally nurturing the next generation of leadership to be ready for the challenge of full responsibility can and must be a priority. If the leader is ever lost, *the show must go on.* A lasting legacy is built on the people who are left when a leader fades from the scene.

For many years, I've had the chance to be associated with one of the greatest engines of talent and leadership development available to college students in America: Students in Free Enterprise (SIFE). SIFE is an organization that complements a student's academic education by providing a real world "laboratory" in which to experiment with entrepreneurship and apply classroom lessons to the dynamics of business experience. Students participate in SIFE through chapters that are chartered at their college or university. They come together as part of a team—part of a real business, actually—and they bring a product or service to market. They use profits from their efforts to drive some kind of charitable project, thus bringing the cycle full circle from entrepreneurial risk, through business execution, the creation of profits and wealth, and eventually, they complete the cycle with philanthropic giving. SIFE provides that practical, *real world* edge to kids who might otherwise fall victim to bookish philosophy and too much theory. SIFE cannot replace the important learning that takes place in the classroom, but it helps to sharpen those lessons; in my view, it is a necessary complement. SIFE is a great source of leadership talent—if you're looking to recruit future leaders to your team, look for students who participate in SIFE. If you can't find someone who experienced SIFE, find someone who's worked their way through school. Spare yourself the pompous, one-dimensional academics. You'll spend their first years teaching them stuff about hard work and life that they should have already learned.

I've always told people that my only job was to find great people, bring them on the team, give them more responsibility than they believe they can handle, give them the tools they need, and then trust them to get the job done and get out of their way. Whether they have experience with SIFE or just a great mix of schooling, working, or extracurricular leadership, we took pride in our ability to bring the best young people on our team and have them achieve great results. Sure, there were plenty of experienced folks around to learn from, and great systems for sharing information, but it all starts with picking the right people.

Hiring a competent team does not mean the leader is off the hook and free to ignore the details of the business. In fact, the leader may need to bring more passion to attacking the details than anyone else (recall the importance of the small things). General Colin Powell has put it this way: "Never neglect details. When everyone's mind is dulled or distracted, the leader must be doubly vigilant." The leader doesn't need to manage all of the details all of the time, but when he or she spots a problem, he or she better be able to dig farther and faster than everyone else.

Jack Shewmaker once told a newly promoted young executive at Manco that he needed "to be a generalist, with the right indicators at hand to manage the broad scale of things. But when something goes wrong," Jack warned, "you need to be a better analyst than the best analyst on your team. You're going to have to wash plenty of doors and windows."

So while a leader needs a great team of managers, he or she sometimes needs to upset the status quo and break some glass. In a sense, the leader is a maverick, setting down the law but then operating around it when need be. In fact, the leader needs mavericks that challenge the system at all levels. The best companies have well-defined, well-managed systems and processes that control standard outcomes, but all systems and processes need mavericks who know how to smash the system when the customer needs something that doesn't fit the script. It is yet another paradox of the kind of leadership that facilitates great performance.

THE COUP DE GRÂCE OF DISCIPLINE: EXECUTION

Everything about a leader—from learning, to vision, to trust, to drive, to caring—boils down to one, glaring demand: the team must *execute*. General Patton said it simply: "Execution is the thing." A team exists for no other reason but to perform and succeed. Discipline pulls all of the elements of leadership together on the field of battle and provides the final tools of execution. Discipline is the time spent sharpening the axe for the single blow that will fell the tree.

In business, execution means profit. Profit is the ultimate measure of whether a vision is worthwhile or whether a team is well led and well managed. Without profit, a company cannot survive, it cannot maintain the team. One of Sam's rules says, "Control your expenses better than your competition." Wal-Mart runs a tighter ship than anybody in the retail business and the results are obvious. Whether you're in a market with thin or fat margins, you need to know your costs and keep them lower than everyone you compete against. Then you'll always have more room to react to change, make investments, reward performers, and the general flexibility it takes to succeed.

I mentioned Manco's two-to-a-room hotel policy earlier, but we replicated that cost control mentality everywhere. Eventually, it took root in the habits and decisions of everyone on the team. In some cases, our habits were so strict that they came to redefine policies that previously had been far more liberal. For instance, we allowed business class air travel for flights over six or seven hours, but as our international travel increased, our troops never took advantage of that provision. The culture overruled the policy and people routinely flew coach class to Europe, only occasionally upgrading to business class or some intermediate service on trips to Asia. Our fanaticism about cost control trickled right down to the way we decorated our facilities. We weren't cheap—we felt that our team deserved nice surroundings—but we subscribed to a design philosophy that, as I mentioned previously, was considered "tastefully poor." We stayed away from extravagance and stuck with simple, clean accommodations. I know for a fact that the discipline we maintained in our surroundings translated into an attitude of cost control throughout our entire company.

Constant challenges forced us to learn our disciplines at Manco. We faced many of our own corporate crucibles through the years, from a crisis of financial management, to a crisis of quality assurance, and a crisis of operational efficiency. In surviving each of these predicaments, we resolved to break bad habits and introduce new disciplines. We installed systems of activity-based management, product engineering, and QA; we made the right investments in our operations team and we gave them the tools they needed. We always made these investments somewhat begrudgingly, fighting our urges to spend our money on sales and marketing in order to reach our customers directly, but we knew that we needed balance and we found that achieving balance is a discipline much like eating healthy and exercising. We learned and relearned a mantra that hung on our walls, drawn from the sport of rowing: "To go fast ... row slowly and in equal rhythm." We learned that our structure needed balance in terms of talent and tools, and somehow maintained the discipline to keep that balance and react quickly when we saw signs of trouble.

One discipline we learned, which crossed all boundaries of the company, was how to measure results and maintain accountability. We expected our leaders to know their areas and be responsible for execution in all aspects. We expected them to report on their performance in daily, weekly, and monthly formats. To emphasize the importance of measuring the business, we hung a quotation from *The One Minute Manager* by Ken Blanchard, which read, "If you can't measure it, you can't manage it." And when faced with problems, we expected our leaders to follow Ross Perot's advice: "When you see a snake, just kill it. Don't form a committee on snakes." In other words, don't freeze with inaction. Solve the problem.

If the problem was bigger than the leader could handle, we expected our entire executive team to know about it and understand it. We expected our leaders to be adept at recognizing and defining problems and potential solutions. My friend Ken Morris, former VP of Product Development at Rubbermaid during its heyday, has said, "A well-defined problem is half solved." If our team invested their time and energy into defining problems, we were far more likely to solve them. Sounds obvious, doesn't it? It isn't. There are too many leaders who aren't patient enough to run a true diagnostic test; they readily justify the "Ready-Fire-Aim!" mentality, which may be crucial to speed, but can be so reckless at the same time. While that mentality suits many situations, when it comes to understanding the problems facing your team, speed is no excuse for sloppiness and poor discipline.

I always found it tough to strike a balance between encouraging risk taking and allowing mistakes and being intolerant of ineffectiveness and holding people accountable for poor performance. Sometimes I found the answer in trusting my gut and following Schwartzkopf's advice to simply "do what's right." But often, I found the answer in the discipline of measuring performance, keeping score, setting clear expectations with my team, and providing consistent feedback.

CONTRADICTORY DISCIPLINES?

The discipline of execution also demands that leaders "seize the day" when opportunities make themselves available. An organization must always remain fleet of foot and in a position to react to a changing world. On the surface, this *carpe diem* philosophy seems to contradict the discipline of planning, but it really doesn't. Think of it as an "override" mechanism. Plans are great, but plans neither define, nor predict the future. Don't make the mistake of viewing a plan as a reality that has yet to happen. Plans are merely projections of what the leader and the team expect to find on the road ahead. If the team encounters unanticipated conditions, that doesn't necessarily mean that the plan was bad, but it does mean that something unexpected happened. This is never the time to embrace your ego and cling to your plan instead of recognizing the reality you have encountered. Admit that you missed something and react appropriately. As General Patton said, "One does not try to make the circumstances fit the plans. One tries to make the plans fit the circumstances." Change the plans, but stick to the strategy and hold the vision.

A great example of sticking to a strategy while changing the plan happened in our business in 1985. That year's budget did not include plans to launch a new category of products—until one of our folks overheard a Wal-Mart buyer talking about the growing small-office trend in retail. The buyer said he would probably buy carton-sealing tape someday from whichever supplier sold him a full line of mailing and shipping supplies.

We suddenly found ourselves racing to protect our core business. We assigned one of our best marketing partners, Kiki Matthews, to lead the charge to launch an entire new product category. Despite our constant focus on speed at the company, I don't think anybody ever matched the standard we set with that project. Within ninety days, we brought a line of *thirty-six* products to market, each one stocked in our warehouse and ready to ship. From Bubble Wrap® (Bubble Wrap® is a registered trademark of The Sealed Air Corporation) to corrugated boxes; from photograph mailers to mailing tubes; from kraft wrapping paper to mailing labels; we introduced a brand new category we called Caremail®.

And thankfully so. Throughout the nineties, much of our profits came from that category as we expanded at Wal-Mart, other major retailers, and into the emerging office mega-store retail channel. Brian Vulpitta took the marketing reins from Kiki almost as soon as the category hit the stores, helping our sales team to quickly achieve a critical mass with Caremail® and firmly establish its permanence. Over the next decade, Caremail® helped fuel our funding of countless products and categories; but just as importantly, it fueled our confidence to branch out and try new things. While the category was not part of our *plan*, defending our turf and growing our business was certainly part of our *strategy*; as was listening to our customers and letting their ideas direct our priorities.

Plans that are rigidly conceived and followed with absolute reverence are the false gods of leadership. In the changing conditions of a world in overdrive, avoid fixed plans and agendas in favor of flexibility. Be open to chance, or as my dad said, "make yourself available to opportunity." In the end, planning remains a discipline, and so does execution, even when circumstances conspire to change your course.

The Servant Leader

"There is only one boss—the customer. And he or she can fire anybody in the company from the Chairman on down, simply by spending his or her money elsewhere."

Sam Walton

I met Mr. Sam about a year after I started selling Wal-Mart. It was early one morning, well before 7:00 a.m. I had gone to Bentonville to visit with our buyer at the time, Joe Craig. Joe was under the gun with some paperwork that needed to be done before Wal-Mart could begin buying new products from Manco, so I came in to help him out.

Joe greeted me in the lobby and we walked back to the office area together. As we turned a corner we nearly ran into Mr. Sam. He was carrying a huge stack of computer printouts. When he saw Joe, he asked him a question. It looked like they were getting into a serious conversation, so I turned around to leave. It was then that Mr. Sam seemed to notice me.

"Hello, young man," he said. "Who are you?"

"Jack Kahl, sir." I turned to face him. I was so nervous, I had to keep myself from shaking visibly.

"Sam Walton," he said, shifting his stack of papers from one arm to another, and sticking his free hand out. Later, Joe told me that the stack of papers Sam held were sales reports. He had come into the office two hours before a meeting with Wal-

Mart's merchandising staff in order to prepare. Joe assured me that Sam would go into the meeting with a better grasp of the facts than anyone else and he would let them have it. Sam had a short-term photographic memory, Joe explained, but he would forget the numbers by nighttime. Sam would only remember the information long enough to drive the team's thinking, demand adjustments, assure accountability, and then he would move on to the next area of his concern.

I took Sam's hand, "Nice to meet you, sir."

"Call me Sam. What are you doing here so early in the morning, Jack?"

"I came in to work with Joe on some paperwork."

Sam laughed. "Well, good luck. Joe's not the best with paperwork." His eyes sparkled at Joe. "We have a lot of buyers down here, Jack. A lot of buyers who are good at paperwork. What we don't have enough of is merchants. But Joe's a merchant. He's one of our best. He's not so good with the paperwork, though."

What could I say? I kept my mouth shut.

Sam smiled a moment longer and then gave me an intense look. "Are we doing enough to help you, son?"

If there is one phrase that encapsulates the spirit of Mr. Sam, that is the one. During my many visits to Wal-Mart, and throughout my correspondence with Sam, he asked me that simple question: "Jack, are we doing enough to help you succeed?" Sam wanted his company to *serve* its vendors and to do whatever it took to help them succeed, because he knew that most vendors would pay this success back in spades. Mr. Sam was a genuine, authentic person who truly cared about his partners; but don't be fooled, he was a shrewd businessman who knew that whatever he gave to his partners, he would receive back many times over. It's been said for thousands of years: *give and you shall receive.* That is the essence of servant leadership.

Sam knew that the only reason a business exists is to achieve a profit, and that the surest path to profit was through a completely satisfied customer. He also knew that an organization is built on its people, and that those people have the power to decide how well the company serves its customers. But you can't just *tell* people that they must serve customers for the sake of the organization, you have to *show* them how and give them the incentives to do it. Over the course of his career, it became clear to Sam that the idea of service wasn't merely about customer service: it was about imbedding a philosophy of service into every member of the team. He came to know that if he served every partner on his team, the *ideal* of service would trickle down to the customer, and this would absolutely translate into business results. People tend to treat others the way they are treated. It sure sounds like Mr. Sam put the "golden rule" to work, doesn't it?

The career of one of my good friends exemplifies servant leadership. This probably won't surprise you: he worked for Wal-Mart. I met Ron Loveless when he was a Merchandise Manager at the company. At the time, he was Joe Craig's boss, the buyer mentioned previously. Ron was the ultimate merchant. It was through his vision that Manco introduced a line of seasonal home insulation products in 1977. His vision sprang from his customer service instincts, and with the energy crisis of that decade in full swing, he knew the product line would be a hit—and it was. I could go on with a bunch of examples of Ron's merchandising and retailing expertise and how he served his customers, but the story of his career is the most compelling example.

Ron's mother was Sam Walton's housekeeper. When Ron finished his tour with the U.S. Air Force, the first call he got welcoming him home was from Mr. Sam. Sam offered Ron a job as a stock boy working in a store for his brother, Bud. Ron, having only a high school degree and already wondering what he would do next, promptly accepted. He liked Mr. Sam, and with his own mother as an example, Ron knew Sam took care of the people who worked for him.

Ron reported to work, and by his own admission he simply did not look the part of a serious associate. Dressed in a white t-shirt and leather jacket *à la* James Dean, he noted a look of suspicion in Bud's eye. Within a few hours, Sam got a call from Bud. The way Ron tells it, Bud said to Sam, "Now Sam, I've always said you're the best damn horse picker there is, but maybe you screwed up this time." All Ron could do was to put his head down and work the way his mother and the USAF had taught him. Three days later, Bud was back on the phone asking his brother for three more like Ron.

Ron's philosophy was simple. He had a strong work ethic, but there was more going on than that: Ron knew that no matter his title, his job was to *serve* everyone who depended on him to do it well. Even though he was "just a stock boy," he would be the best damned stock boy Sam Walton had ever hired. Ron's philosophy of service *served* him well. His career progressed from stock boy, to Department Salesman, to Department Manager, to Assistant Store Manager, to Store Manager, to Buyer, to Merchandise Manager, to Vice President of Merchandising.

Ron earned the VP position after volunteering to write the company's first purchasing manual for Jack Shewmaker, Wal-Mart's President at the time. Volunteering for assignments like that—assignments that nobody else wanted—earned Ron the respect of his leaders. They came to trust him as someone truly committed to serving the needs of the business.

I would be remiss if I failed to mention that Mr. Sam eventually went to Ron and asked him to head up a new business for the company: a new concept called a "wholesale club." You may have heard of it, it's called Sam's Club. Ron knew assignments such as these could send a top manager right out the door if they failed, but he accepted the challenge all the same. Subsequently, he earned a permanent spot in the annals of corporate America by starting the first company to ever achieve $1 billion in revenues after just two years in business and to never post a loss.

Ron achieved much in his career, all with just a high school degree. But he clearly brought a heck of a dose of hard work and street smarts. And there is no doubt that much of his success came from his willingness to serve in order to lead.

MANCO T. DUCK

Somewhere on our winding road, we had the grand idea of branding Manco's flagship product—duct tape—with a fuzzy yellow duck. (Mostly because people always pronounced it "duck" tape.) I am forever grateful to John Nottingham and John Spirk, longtime friends of mine, for firmly establishing the look and personality of our duck icon. Their knowledge of psychology and their wizardry of design brought a character named Manco Duck to life. Along the way, we added the middle initial "T," which stands for Trust. We felt that the basis of our entire business revolved around relationships, and as I've already said, relationships are built on trust.

Aside from phonetics, there was another, even greater reason for our investment in Manco Duck. The Duck was friendly. The Duck was helpful. We called him our "Dale Carnegie in feathers," thus alluding to the great behaviorist who taught countless salespeople how to build relationships with his book, *How to Win Friends and Influence People*. But aside from all of his endearing traits, the Duck was, most importantly, a *servant*.

Duck® Tape is the ultimate servant: it does whatever the customer wants it to do. Its countless uses range from the immensely practical, to the unthinkable, to the utterly absurd. It's a fun product, but with its low cost and its ability to salvage broken things (or prevent them from breaking in the first place), it is the guardian angel of material goods.

In the early 1980s, we spent $10,000 we didn't have on some market research to gauge the idea of branding our product with a duck. The experts told us not to do it: men buy duct tape, they said, and there is no way they would be partial to a yellow duck. We ignored their advice, despite our deep desire to get something for the pricey investment.

What's interesting is that these so-called experts missed two things: First, that Manco Duck symbolized the friendly flexibility of a product that is willing to sit in a toolbox until the prepared do-it-yourselfer reaches for it as a last resort. And second, that Wal-Mart and other retailers would transform the face of retailing and bring more women into the hardware department. (To their credit, the "experts" did say that women were less averse to a duck than men.)

But as important as Manco Duck has been to our company as a symbol of servant leadership, he only came onstage after that crucial element had become embedded in our corporate psyche. Long before the Duck's first image was sketched, we were the first duct tape distributor to recommend that duct tape be packaged in shrink-wrap. When we first came on the scene, duct tape was sold as unpackaged rolls. Imagine our gall: we proposed adding cost to a commodity! Why? Because the rolls often stuck together on the shelf and customers had a tough time prying them apart. We saw the value of bringing some convenience to the consumer and relieving them of a struggle in the aisle. We knew that serving customers was a *value proposi-*

tion—and value was not always determined by low cost. We stole the mantra that there is "no such thing as a commodity" from one of one of our key suppliers, the Sealed Air Corporation, and their long-time leader, Dermot Dunphy. In an industry that basically combined paper and air into protective packaging products, Dermot taught his troops that service excellence—and sometimes a small dose of extra cost—can bring the peace of mind or ease of experience that customers are looking for. It's not *all* about cost, it's about value. Understanding value from the eyes of the customer became our battle cry, and Manco T. Duck became our Paul Revere, always shouting to rally our team against 3M.

SERVANT LEADERSHIP

The ultimate job of the leader is to serve his or her team. Servant leadership is the beginning and end point of effective leadership; it is the alpha and the omega. Consider how the idea of service is embedded in all of the elements of leadership I've described in this book:

- Character: You serve your team with credibility, integrity, and the core values that they expect; and from the *edge* that comes of self-respect and self-confidence.

- Learning: You serve your team by being a student, by setting aside your *ego* and acquiring the knowledge required for success.

- Creativity: You serve your team by crafting a vision they understand and are inspired and motivated to follow.

- Drive: You serve your team by bringing the passion and *energy* that it takes to stand above the crowd.

- Courage: You serve your team by taking risks and standing up to your fears.

- Caring: You care for and motivate your team by understanding their needs as human beings.

- Discipline: You serve your team by maintaining discipline and focus, and by providing the management tools that are essential to *execution* and success.

I italicized four words above: edge, ego, energy, and execution. In General Electric's 2000 Annual Report, Jack Welch described the four E's that GE looks for in its developing leaders: the *energy* "to cope with the frenetic pace of change"; the ability to *energize*, and "galvanize the organization and inspire it to action"; the *edge*, or the self-confidence to make the tough calls"; and the ability to *execute*—to always deliver and never disappoint. No matter how a writer, teacher, or leader chooses to categorize and summarize the traits or elements of leadership, they all seem to revolve around the same theme: leading others is about serving others.

A servant leader is pervasively present through the many elements that define his or her skill as a leader but is wondrously imperceptible at the same time. It is the ultimate paradox of leadership. Lao-tze, a sixth century Chinese philosopher, said it best: "A leader is best when people barely know he exists. Not so good when people obey and acclaim him. Worse when they despise him. But of a good leader who talks little, when his work is done and his aim fulfilled, they will say, 'We did it ourselves.'"

The job of the leader is to grow leaders at all levels, to obsolete himself for the benefit of others and the organization.

The only true measure of success for a leader is the creation of a legacy that survives his absence.

Robert Woodruff, former president of Coca-Cola, said pretty much the same thing as Lao-tze: "Man can accomplish great success if he doesn't care who gets the credit." From the choice to learn to the choice to serve, self-interest has no place on the team. Many leaders certainly bring an ego to various aspects of their lives; it is an inevitable weakness of humanity to get caught up in the trophies, trappings, and the need to proclaim our success to others; but the most effective leader sets these egotistical tendencies aside.

SERVING FROM THE HEART

Throughout literary history, the human heart has been a metaphor for emotional thinking. It's often said that our "heart" balances our rational brains, but I think our hearts are more than just a counterweight. I think our emotions complete us and give meaning to our rational minds—emotion is, after all, a part of our overall intelligence. Our hearts are at the root of all of our choices, including the choice to step up and lead. Whether driven by a selfish ambition or a selfless hope for the success of others, emotion is behind the choice to take command. It's best that we recognize our desire, our emotion, our heart, so that we can engage it. By recognizing what is at the heart of our choice to lead, we will be better able to express it and transfer it to our team. Only by *leading from the heart* can we fully engage the power of our humanity and the passion of our team. Only by leading from the heart are we true to the core of our motivation.

While the emergence of leadership is rife with complexity and its expression in people as varied as the stars in the sky, the root is beautiful and simple. Leading is about making a choice in your heart to help, coach, and serve others. Leading from the heart is the only path to serving the team. And when the well-served team wins success, they will find that their servant is their master.

APPENDIX:

SAM'S RULES FOR BUILDING A BUSINESS:

RULE 1: COMMIT to your business. Believe in it more than anybody else. I think I overcame every single one of my personal shortcomings by the sheer passion I brought to my work. I don't know if you're born with this kind of passion, or if you can learn it. But I do know you need it. If you love your work, you'll be out there every day trying to do it best you possibly can, and pretty soon everybody around will catch the passion from you—like a fever.

RULE 2: SHARE your profits with all your associates, and treat them as partners. In turn, they will treat you as a partner, and together you will all perform beyond your wildest expectations. Remain a corporation and retain control if you like, but behave as a servant leader in a partnership. Encourage your associates to hold a stake in the company. Offer discounted stock, and grant them stock for their retirement. It's the single best thing we ever did.

RULE 3: MOTIVATE your partners. Money and ownership alone aren't enough. Constantly, day by day, think of new and more interesting ways to motivate and challenge your partners. Set high goals, encourage competition, and then keep score. Make bets with outrageous payoffs. If things get stale, cross-pollinate; have mangers switch jobs with one another to stay challenged. Keep everybody guessing as to what your next trick is going to be. Don't become predictable.

RULE 4: COMMUNICATE everything you possibly can to your partners. The more they know, the more they'll understand. The more they understand, the more they'll care. Once they care, there's no stopping them. If you don't trust your associates to know what's going on, they'll know you don't really consider them partners. Information is power, and the gain you get from empowering your associates more than offsets the risk of informing your competitors.

RULE 5: APPRECIATE everything your associates do for the business. A paycheck and a stock option will buy one kind of loyalty. But all of us like to be told how much somebody appreciates what we do for them. We like to hear it often, and especially when we have done something we're really proud of. Nothing else can quite substitute for a few well-chosen, well-timed, sincere words of praise. They're absolutely free—and worth a fortune.

RULE 6: CELEBRATE your success. Find some humor in your failures. Don't take yourself so seriously. Loosen up, and everybody around you will loosen up. Have fun. Show enthusiasm—always. When all else fails, put on a costume and sing a silly song. Then make everybody else sing with you. Don't do a hula on Wall Street. It's been done. Think up your own stunt. All of this is more important, and more fun, than you think, and it really fools the competition. "Why should we take those cornballs at Wal-Mart seriously?"

RULE 7: LISTEN to everyone in your company. And figure out ways to get them talking. The folks on the front lines—the ones who actually talk to the customer—are the only ones who really know what's going on out there. You'd better find out

ABOUT THE AUTHORS

Jack Kahl was the owner and CEO of Manco, Inc. for nearly thirty years. He sits on multiple boards and splits his time between writing, speaking, and consulting. He lives in Avon Lake, Ohio. This is his first book.

Tom Donelan worked at Manco for Jack Kahl for more than ten years. He is currently a vice president with a northeast Ohio manufacturer, and he lives in Strongsville, Ohio, with his wife and three young children.

Visit us online at www.jackkahl.com

what they know. This really is what total quality is all about. To push responsibility down in your organization and to force good ideas to bubble up within it, you must listen to what your associates are trying to tell you.

RULE 8: EXCEED your customer's expectations. If you do, they'll come back over and over. Give them what they want—and a little more. Let them know you appreciate them. Make good on all your mistakes and don't make excuses—apologize. Stand behind everything you do. The two most important words I ever wrote were on that first Wal-Mart sign: "Satisfaction Guaranteed." They're still up there, and they have made all the difference.

RULE 9: CONTROL your expenses better than your competition. This is where you can always find the competitive advantage. For twenty-five years running—long before Wal-Mart was known as the nation's largest retailer—we ranked number one in our industry for the lowest ratio of expenses to sales. You can make a lot of different mistakes and still recover if you run an efficient operation. Or you can be brilliant and still go out of business if you're too inefficient.

RULE 10: SWIM upstream. Go the other way. Ignore the conventional wisdom. If everybody else is doing it one way, there's a good chance you can find your niche by going in exactly the opposite direction. But be prepared for a lot of folks to wave you down and tell you you're headed the wrong way. I guess in all my years what I heard more often than anything was: a town of less than 50,000 population cannot support a discount store for very long.

www.ingramcontent.com/pod-product-compliance
Lightning Source LLC
Chambersburg PA
CBHW021111210326
41598CB00017B/1409